UPGRADE

3

Editora: Gisele Aga

1ª edição
2012

Richmond

Richmond

Diretoria: *Paul Berry*
Gerência editorial: *Sandra Possas*
Coordenação de edição de texto: *Gisele Aga*
Coordenação de arte: *Christiane Borin*
Coordenação de pesquisa iconográfica: *Ana Lucia Soares*
Coordenação de *bureau*: *Américo Jesus*
Coordenação de revisão: *Adriana Cristina Bairrada, Elaine Cristina del Nero*
Coordenação de produção gráfica: *André Monteiro, Maria de Lourdes Rodrigues*
Coordenação de produção industrial: *Wilson Troque*

Coordenação do projeto: *Gisele Aga*

Edição de texto: *Gisele Aga*
Assistência editorial: *Adriana Beatriz Saporito, Ana Lucia Militello*
Preparação: *Maria Estela de Alcântara*
Revisão: *Augusto de Salvo Russo, Beatriz Pinto Semprini, Miguel Silva, Rafael Gustavo Spigel, Vivian Marques Viccino*
Edição de arte: *Andreza Moreira*
Projeto gráfico: *Andreza Moreira*
Capa: *Andreza Moreira*
Pesquisa iconográfica: *Felipe Campos, Mariana Lima*
Tratamento de imagens: *Fabio N. Precendo, Alexandre Petreca, Pix Art*
Editoração eletrônica: *Aeroestudio*
Pré-impressão: *Hélio P. de Souza Filho, Marcio Hideyuki Kamoto*
Impressão e acabamento: *Ricargraf*

Manual do professor: *Izaura Valverde, Luciana de Oliveira Silva*

Equipe de redação: *Ana Rosa Marinho Oliveira Vivarini, Carla Maurício Coelho da Silva Vianna, Claudia Priore, Cristina Lanza, Daniella Bergamo, Eliane Calza, Heloisa Helena Soares Quirino, João Rodrigo Lima Agildo, Luciana S. Pinheiro, Marcelo Furlin, Renata Monteiro Mendes*

Dados Internacionais de Catalogação na Publicação (CIP)
(Câmara Brasileira do Livro, SP, Brasil)

Upgrade 3 / editora Gisele Aga. — 1. ed. —
São Paulo: Moderna, 2012. — (Upgrade)

1. Inglês - Estudo e ensino I. Aga, Gisele.
II. Série.

12-06582 CDD-420.7

Índices para catálogo sistemático:
1. Inglês: Estudo e ensino 420.7

ISBN 978-85-16-08030-3 (LA)
ISBN 978-85-16-08031-0 (LP)

RICHMOND PUBLISHING
EDITORA MODERNA LTDA.
Rua Padre Adelino, 758 - Belenzinho
São Paulo - SP - Brasil - CEP 03303-904
Central de atendimento ao usuário: 0800 771 8181
Fax +55 11 2790-1284
www.richmond.com.br
2013

Impresso no Brasil

Contents

In the Job Market

FOODPIX / GETTY IMAGES

RAFAEL GENTILE

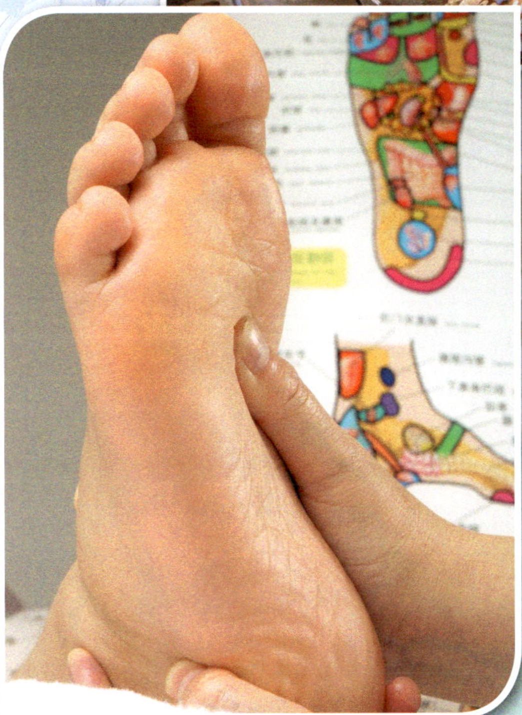

DOTWEB / SHUTTERSTOCK

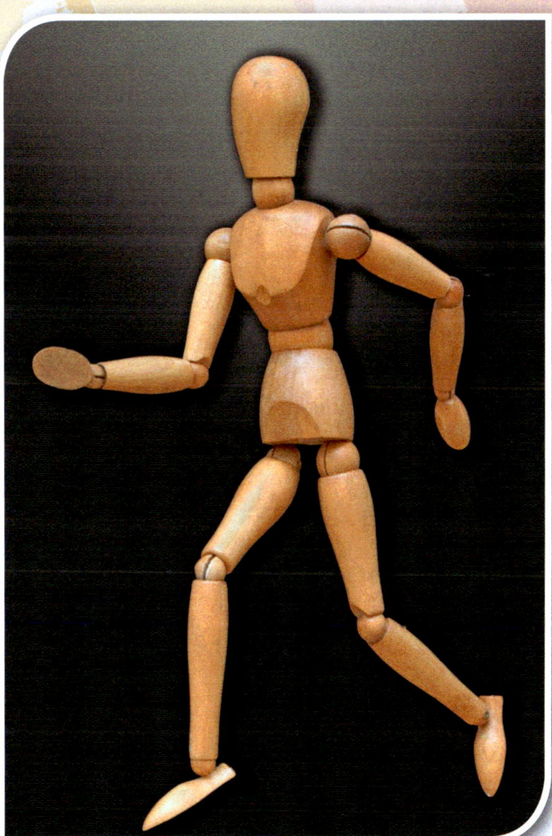

ROB WILKINSON / ALAMY / OTHER IMAGES

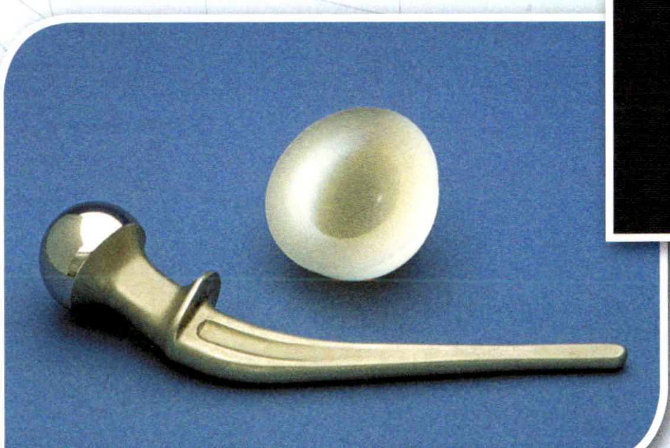

PHIL DEGGINGER / ALAMY / OTHER IMAGES

Quiz

HOW MUCH DO YOU KNOW ABOUT THE JOB MARKET?

1

What is the mannequin on page 5 used for?

a [ ] crash tests
b [ ] hanging jewelry
c [x] basing drawings on its positions
d [ ] fitting clothes
e [ ] use as a toy

2

Each part of our body is reflected in some part of our feet. What part(s) of the body is/are reflected in our toes?

a [x] spine
b [ ] lung and chest
c [ ] heart
d [ ] lower back
e [ ] brain and head

RAFAEL GENTILE

3

What is the name of the communications professional who is employed by a media source in one country and stationed in a foreign land to cover government, religion, and other matters?

a [ ] investigative reporter
b [ ] news journalist
c [ ] public-relations specialist
d [ ] broadcast journalist
e [x] foreign correspondent

4

Which one of these treats is not typically Brazilian?

a [ ] paçoca
b [ ] brigadeiro
c [ ] maria-mole
d [x] madalena
e [ ] beijinho

5

Which alternative shows one single Brazilian university that does not run its own publishing house?

a ☐ FGV (SP); UFPR (PR); UFRJ (RJ)

b ☐ PUC (MG); São Francisco (SP); Unisinos (RS)

c ☐ UFRN (RN); PUC-RJ (RJ); Unicamp (SP)

d ☐ UFPE (PE); Unip (SP); UFRGS (RS)

e ☐ USP (SP); UnB (GO); Uneb (BA)

6

Which of these acronyms is related to health care?

BP BPM ER

a ☐ Bachelor of Philosophy; Business Process Management; Erbium (chemical element)

b ☐ Blood Pressure; Beats Per Minute; Emergency Room

c ☐ Blood Pressure; Business Process Management; Emergency Room

d ☐ Bachelor of Philosophy; Beats Per Minute; Erbium (chemical element)

e ☐ Blood Pressure; Beats Per Minute; Erbium (chemical element)

RAFAEL GENTILE

7

What is the most common type of prosthesis?

a ☐ Dental prosthesis

b ☐ Prosthetic arm

c ☐ Prosthetic foot

d ☐ Silicone implants

e ☐ Prosthetic vertebrae

8

A coroner is...

a ☐ a mental health doctor that uses the creative process of making art to improve and enhance the well-being of individuals of all ages.

b ☐ a doctor who works to find the cause of deaths that are accidental, violent, or unexplained.

c ☐ a medical doctor who examines tissue samples and performs autopsies to find clues about the cause of death when a crime is suspected.

d ☐ a medical professional who assesses patient's state of physical health by the color and contours of their eyes.

e ☐ a doctor whose job is to evaluate and treat patients with disorders of the visual system.

1 Ethical Decision-Making

PRE-READING

Look at the picture. What's the relation between the sentence on the board and the picture itself?

What Does It Mean to Be a Citizen?

The question "What does it mean to be a citizen?" has no simple answer. On a purely-definition based description, what it means to be a citizen is that a person is a legally recognized inhabitant of the country he or she lives in. In the UK, this means the person pays taxes and is entitled to the help of the benefits and NHS systems. However, in practice, answering the question "What does it mean to be a citizen?" is far from easy. As new rules and tests for people wanting British citizenship show, being a citizen is about far more than a legal status. It is about understanding and accepting and being a part of the culture, rather than an observer from the outside. [...]

Extracted from <http://www.responsiblecitizen.co.uk/What-it-means-to-be-a-citizen.html>. Accessed on February 1, 2010.

NHS (National Health Service) systems: sistemas de saúde
UK (United Kingdom): Reino Unido

After Reading

1 Look at the picture on page 8 again and answer the questions in Portuguese.

a O que a maioria dos alunos está tentando fazer?

b Por que os alunos têm essa atitude?

c Qual é a sua opinião em relação à atitude dos alunos?

2 Answer the questions based on the text.

a What does it mean to be a citizen?

b What does a person in the UK do to be recognized as a citizen?

3 Leia o extrato de texto abaixo e discuta-o com seus colegas.

> "A moral é o conjunto de regras de conduta assumidas livre e conscientemente pelos indivíduos, com a finalidade de organizar as relações interpessoais segundo os valores do bem e do mal.
>
> A ética, ou filosofia moral, é mais abstrata, constituindo a parte da filosofia que se ocupa com a reflexão sobre as noções e os princípios que fundamentam a vida moral.
>
> Por exemplo, são questões éticas indagar a respeito do que é o bem e do que é o mal, o que são valores, qual a natureza do dever, em que consiste a moral autônoma, qual a finalidade da ação moral, e assim por diante. As respostas a essas e outras indagações caracterizam as diversas concepções de vida moral elaboradas pelos filósofos no decorrer dos tempos. […]"

RAFAEL GENTILE

Extraído de ARANHA, Ana Lúcia de Arruda & MARTINS, Maria Helena Pires, *Temas de Filosofia*. São Paulo: Moderna, 2005, p. 218.

a Baseado nas informações acima, analise o comportamento dos alunos na imagem da página 8.

b Que outras atitudes do cotidiano se assemelham àquela expressa pelos alunos na página 8?

c O que podemos e devemos fazer para sermos mais éticos em nosso dia a dia?

Vocabulary in Use

1 Match the words below with their definitions.

a citizen

b citizenship

c far more than

d taxes

e entitled

f rather than

(D) a sum of money demanded by a government for its support or for specific facilities or services

(e) to have a title, right, or claim to something

(A) an inhabitant of a city or town

(b) the status, rights, and duties of a citizen, especially of a particular country

(F) to indicate negation as a contrary choice or wish

( ) an amount or number that is larger than another

2 Replace the words in bold in the sentences below. Use words from exercise 1. Make changes, if necessary.

a The **duties** on gas have been raised.

the taxes on gas have been raised

b People who are **allowed** to vote should arrive on time.

People who are entitled to vote should arrive on time

c That country's first **inhabitants** arrived there in the 17th century.

that country's first citizen arrived there in the 17th century

d Claire called off the wedding **instead of** admitting that she doesn't love him anymore.

Claire called off the wedding rather than admitting that she doesn't love him anymore

e Frank is applying for his American **green card**.

Frank is applying for his American citizenship

f The manager created **a lot of** problems when I went there to solve the ones I already had.

the manager created far more than problems when I went there to solve the ones I already had

3 Como vimos na unidade 4 do volume 2, *linking words* são palavras ou expressões que estabelecem ligações entre orações. Observe:

However, in practice, answering the question "What does it mean to be a citizen?" is far from easy.

However indica contraste.

Outras *linking words* que indicam contraste são:

- **although:** embora
- **unlike:** diferentemente de
- **in spite of:** a despeito de
- **whereas:** ao passo que
- **nevertheless:** apesar disso

Now complete the sentences below using the linking words above.

a The old stadium was fairly simple, ______________ the new stadium is really sophisticated.

b ______________ in poor health, my dad continued to carry out his duties.

c This is a simple process. ______________, there are dangers.

d ______________ most people at school, I come to school by bus.

e What you said was true. It was impolite ______________.

f We went to the game ______________ yesterday's heavy rain.

Appendix 1 page 150

Grammar in Use

CONDITIONAL SENTENCES (IF CLAUSES)

Conditional sentences são orações que expressam condições. Apresentam diferentes combinações de tempos verbais e vêm relacionadas a orações principais.

Zero Conditional

Utilizado para falar sobre uma verdade universal ou para dar uma ordem ou instrução.	If you **heat** (Simple Present) water to 100 °C, it **boils** (Simple Present). If you **need** (Simple Present) help, **call** (Imperative) me.

First Conditional

Utilizado para expressar uma ação possível de acontecer no futuro.	If she **comes** (Simple Present) earlier, she **will meet** (Simple Future) him. If they **don't study** (Simple Present), they **won't have** (Simple Future) good grades.

Second Conditional

Utilizado para expressar uma ação que não é real ou não é provável de acontecer.	If I **had** money, I **would lend** you some. Simple Past / would + verb We **wouldn't be** lost if we **bought** a map. would + verb / Simple Past

Notas

If pode ser usado no início da frase ou no meio das duas partes da frase. Observe o uso ou não da vírgula.	**If** he pays me, I'll iron his shirts for him. They'll wash the car **if** it doesn't rain.
Na linguagem informal, em frases com **if**, **was** é mais utilizado do que **were**. Na linguagem formal, **were** é mais comum que **was**.	If she **was** my mother, I would forgive her. The teacher would choose me if I **weren't** a bad student.
Unless pode ser usado em lugar de **if... not**.	**If we don't** do something now, global warming will get worse. **Unless** we do something now, global warming will get worse.

1 Rewrite the sentences below, replacing the underlined expressions. Use the words in parentheses. The first one is done for you.

a They won't let her into the concert <u>if she doesn't have a ticket</u>. (unless)
They won't let her into the concert unless she has a ticket.

b We will go to the mountains on the weekend <u>unless it rains</u>. (if)
We will go to the mountains on the weekend if it not rain

c <u>Unless you pay for the broken window</u>, I'll call the police. (if)
if you not pay for the broken window, I'll call the police.

d The doctor will not see you <u>if you do not call in advance</u>. (unless)
The doctor will not see you unless call in advance.

2 Read some of the dilemmas teens like Jennifer usually face. Rewrite the dilemmas, using conditional sentences. The first one is done for you.

JUPITER UNLIMITED / IMAGEPLUS

a Jennifer knows her parents won't let her go to the party if they find out the host's parents are not in town. Should Jennifer tell her parents the truth?

If Jennifer tells her parents the host's parents are not in town, they won't let her go to the party.

b Jennifer's best friend is taking part in some risky behavior, such as smoking. Should Jennifer advise her about the health problems she may have?

If jennifer doesn't advise her to the heath problems probably he is going have a câncer

c One of the girls in Jennifer's class has turned against her and is now telling the other girls to bully and isolate her. Should Jennifer talk to the girl or should she ignore her?

If jennifer ignore her, the other girl should ignore her too

d Pamela, who is Jennifer's favorite cousin, has an eating disorder. Jennifer is very sad about this. Pamela's parents don't worry about Pamela at all, but Jennifer and a few friends are concerned. Should Jennifer ask Pamela to see a doctor?

If she ask pamela to see a doctor, she should be fine

3 Underline the correct form to make conditional sentences.

a If you **pour** / **would pour** oil on water, the oil floats.

b If I see Mark tomorrow, I **tell** / **will tell** him the news.

c We **won't travel** / **wouldn't travel** by train if the ticket prices go up.

d I would go to the movies with you if you **got** / **would get** here in time.

e Ice melts if we **will heat** / **heat** it.

f If you **visit** / **will visit** Florianópolis, you will have a great time.

g If we **had had** / **had** longer vacations, we would go to Paris.

4 Circle the conditional sentences in the comic strips below.

A

B

C

5 Write the correct verb forms. Use the words in parentheses and the cues given.

a I ______________ happy if I ______________ my exams. (be – neg.; pass – neg.)

b If we ______________ in making the transition to all-electric vehicles for all transport, we ______________ basically ______________ global energy consumption in half. (succeed; cut)

c If a black cat ______________ your path, you ______________ bad luck. (cross; have)

d ______________ you ______________ to the Moon if someone ______________ you to? (go; ask)

e If there ______________ enough food for the guests to eat, we ______________ some Chinese take-away. (be – neg.; buy)

f I ______________ taxes if I ______________ the president. (lower; be)

g Unless she ______________, she ______________ in time. (hurry up; arrive – neg.)

h If you ______________ anything, ______________. (need; ask)

i If you ______________ harder, you ______________. (try – neg.; fail)

j They said they ______________ home if it ______________. (stay; rain)

6 Complete with a suitable phrase to form conditional sentences.

a We'll cook lunch for everyone if ______________________________.

b If you didn't get to the party early, ______________________________.

c If I have time today, ______________________________.

d You wouldn't sleep very well if ______________________________.

e House plants die if we ______________________________.

f If I were you, ______________________________.

g You will catch a cold unless ______________________________.

7 Answer the questions below with complete sentences.

What would you do if...?

a you needed to write something down and you didn't have a pencil?

____

b you had a bad toothache?

____

c you wanted to go to a concert but you didn't have enough money?

____

Reading

The Hare and the Tortoise

The hare was once boasting of his speed before the other animals. "I have never yet been beaten," said he, "when I put forth my full speed. I challenge any one here to race with me."

The tortoise said quietly, "I accept your challenge."

"That is a good joke," said the hare. "I could dance round you all the way."

"Keep your boasting till you've beaten me," answered the tortoise. "Shall we race?"

So a course was fixed and a start was made. The hare darted almost out of sight at once, but soon stopped and, to show his contempt for the tortoise, lay down to have a nap. The tortoise plodded on and plodded on, and when the hare awoke from his nap, he saw the tortoise just near the winning-post and could not run up in time to save the race.

Then said the tortoise, "Plodding wins the race."

Moral: "Slow and steady progress wins the race."

Extracted from <http://www.aesops-fables.org.uk/aesop-fable-the-hare-and-the-tortoise.htm>. Accessed on February 12, 2010.

ILLUSTRATION: MILTON RODRIGUES ALVES; ART: RAFAEL GENTILE

challenge: desafio
contempt: desprezo
darted: correu rapidamente
hare: lebre
lay down: deitou-se
nap: soneca, cochilo
put forth: mostrar por completo
steady: constante

The Lion and the Mouse

ILLUSTRATION: MILTON RODRIGUES ALVES; ART: RAFAEL GENTILE

Once when a lion was asleep, a little mouse began running up and down upon him. This soon wakened the lion, who placed his huge paw upon the mouse, and opened his big jaws to swallow him.

"Pardon, O King," cried the little mouse. "Forgive me this time, and I shall never forget it. Who knows what I may be able to do for you in turn one of these days?"

The lion was so tickled at the idea of the mouse being able to help him that he lifted up his paw and let him go.

Sometime later the lion was caught in a trap and the hunters who desired to carry him alive to the king tied him to a tree while they went in search of a wagon to carry him on. Just then the little mouse happened to pass by, and seeing the sad plight of the lion he went up to him and soon gnawed away the ropes that bound the king of the beasts.

"Was I not right?" said the little mouse.

Moral: "Small friends may prove to be great friends."

Extracted from <http://www.aesops-fables.org.uk/aesop-fable-the-lion-and-the-mouse.htm>. Accessed on February 12, 2010.

gnawed away: roeu
jaws: mandíbulas
paw: pata
ropes: cordas
swallow: engolir
trap: armadilha
wagon: carroça

After Reading

1 The sentences below refer to the fables. Write T (true), F (false), or NM (not mentioned).

a (F) The hare was not used to winning races.

b (F) The tortoise had tried to beat the hare before.

c (T) The hare was defeated by his own excessive confidence.

d (T) The mouse asked the lion for a second chance when the lion wanted to kill him.

e (T) The moral of *The Lion and the Mouse* is that real friends always help each other.

2 Read the sentences below. They are extracted from the fables. Choose the best synonym for the words in bold.

2.1 "The hare was once **boasting** of his speed before the other animals."

a (   ) lastimando
b (X) vangloriando-se
c (   ) queixando-se
d (   ) chorando

2.2 "The tortoise **plodded on** and **plodded on**, and when the hare awoke from his nap, he saw the tortoise just near the winning-post [...]"

a (   ) andou rapidamente
b (   ) andou
c (   ) correu rapidamente
d (   ) caminhou lentamente

2.3 "Just then the little mouse happened to pass by, and seeing the **sad plight** of the lion [...]"

a (   ) apuro
b (   ) depressão
c (   ) infelicidade
d (   ) tranquilidade

2.4 "The lion was so **tickled** at the idea of the mouse being able to help him that he lifted up his paw and let him go."

a (   ) magoado
b (   ) indiferente
c (   ) entretido
d (   ) contrariado

3 Read the dictionary entry and do the activity.

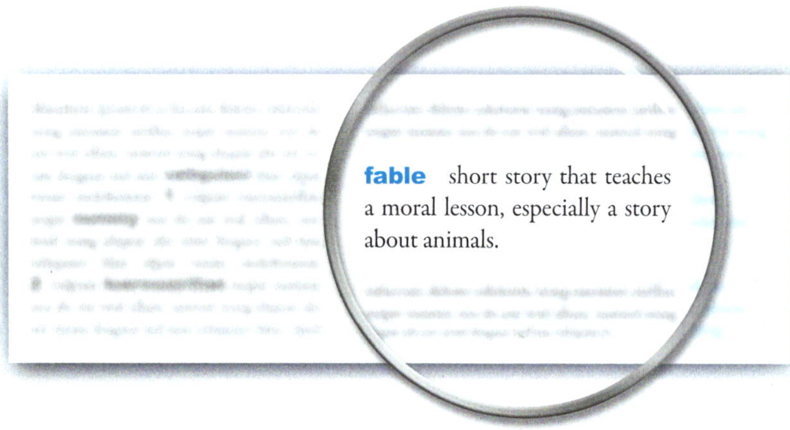

ANDREZA MOREIRA

Longman Dictionary of Contemporary English. 4. ed. London: Longman, 2003. p. 558.

Nas fábulas, os personagens são quase sempre animais. São personagens simbólicos que pensam, sentem e agem como homens; são verdadeiras personificações do ser humano.

Leia novamente as fábulas nas páginas 16 e 17 e verifique qual animal melhor representa cada uma das características abaixo.

a vanity ________________
b determination ________________
c thankfulness ________________
d contempt ________________
e persistence ________________
f courage ________________

Consultando outras fontes

filmes: *Uma segunda chance* (EUA, 1991; direção: Mike Nichols)
O preço de uma verdade (EUA, 2003; direção: Billy Ray)

livro: *Aprendiz do futuro – Cidadania hoje e amanhã* (Ática; autor: Gilberto Dimenstein)

Visual Artist

PHOTO: IMAGEBROKER / ALAMY / OTHER IMAGES; ART: FAFAEL GENTILE

If you are very creative and like to express your feelings and emotions by drawing, then you should make a career out of it. You should consider becoming a visual artist.

Visual artists use many different methods – such as illustration and painting – and a great variety of materials – including pencils, clay, oils, acrylics, or even computers – to express their thoughts and create their artwork, no matter how abstract or stylized that piece of work might be. They match lines, space, perspective, and color in the attempt to produce all the effects necessary to express their perceptions, thoughts, criticism, and sensibility. These professionals study different techniques to improve their performance and their artwork.

As a visual artist you can work as a generalist, which means you will create all different kinds of art (sculptures, drawings, photographs, etc.), or you can pick one artistic expression to specialize in. For instance, you can work with paintings only, or illustrations, or even become a cartoonist.

A visual artist can work in research institutions, studios, ateliers, museums, advertisement agencies, publishing houses, or wherever else he or she chooses. The visual artist can also teach or even have his or her own studio.

In order to become a certified visual artist, one has to take a four-year long college course.

Based on <http://www.belasartes.br/cursos/?curso=artes-visuais>; <http://www.unesp.br/guia/artes_visuais.php>; <http://www.puc-campinas.edu.br/graduacao/cursos/curso.aspx?curs=28>; <http://online.onetcenter.org/link/summary/27-1013.00>; <http://www.careerplanner.com/Job-Outlook/Artists-and-Related-Workers.cfm>. Accessed on February 2, 2010.

clay: argila
criticism: crítica
in the attempt to: na tentativa de
publishing houses: editoras

Você gostaria de ser artista visual? Por quê? / Por que não?

Additional Practice

For exercises 1 to 9, choose the best alternative.

1 U.S. presidents stay in the White House for eight years if they are lucky. Even then, their power wanes considerably in their second term, as George Bush is finding out.
The Iraq war has ________ at his popularity while Hurricane Katrina has savaged his reputation as much as it has ravaged New Orleans.
[...]

Extracted from <http://www.guardian.co.uk/news/blog/2005/sep/05/supremecourt1>. Accessed on March 1, 2010.

a ( ) put forth
b ( ) plodded on
c ( ) gnawed away
d ( ) laid down
e ( ) lifted up

2 It's better to ________ to reach your goal than to do things without thinking.

a ( ) put forth
b ( ) plod on
c ( ) gnaw away
d ( ) lay down
e ( ) lift up

3 We all want to read more about the kidnapping case, but no news has been ________.

a ( ) put forth
b ( ) plod on
c ( ) gnaw away
d ( ) lay down
e ( ) lift up

4 Three big stones needed to be removed, but I couldn't ________ any of them. They were too heavy!

a ( ) put forth
b ( ) plod on
c ( ) gnaw away
d ( ) lay down
e ( ) lift up

5 When Elias arrived home, he told his wife he was so tired he didn't want to have dinner. He went to his bedroom, ________, and slept all night.

a ( ) put forth
b ( ) plodded on
c ( ) gnawed away
d ( ) lay down
e ( ) lifted up

6 Mark, you know I hate when you forget our wedding anniversary! If you...

a ( ) does that again, I'll ask for a divorce!
b ( ) do that again, ask for a divorce!
c ( ) did that again, I'll ask for a divorce!
d ( ) do that again, I'll ask for a divorce!
e ( ) do that again, I'll not ask for a divorce!

7 All my books are autobiographical. If you...

a ( ) read *Fifteen Minutes Away*, then you learn about my childhood.
b ( ) read *Fifteen Minutes Away*, then you would learn about my childhood.
c ( ) will read *Fifteen Minutes Away*, then you learned about my childhood.
d ( ) didn't read *Fifteen Minutes Away*, then you learned about my childhood.
e ( ) don't read *Fifteen Minutes Away*, then you will learn about my childhood.

8 I was totally prepared for that job interview. I was sure that...

a ( ) if they ask me something about the company, I would be able to answer without a doubt.

b ( ) if they will ask me something about the company, I would be able to answer without a doubt.

c ( ) if they ask me something about the company, I will be able to answer without a doubt.

d (X) if they asked me something about the company, I would be able to answer without a doubt.

e ( ) if they would ask me something about the company, I would be able to answer without a doubt.

9 My aunt lives on a farm. When I asked her if she thought it would rain that day, she answered, "You know what they say. If ________."

a ( ) birds will fly low, you will expect rain to fall and wind to blow.

b ( ) birds would fly low, expect rain to fall and a blow.

c ( ) birds fly low, you would expect rain to fall and wind to blow.

d ( ) birds fly low, expect rain to fall and wind to blow.

e ( ) birds fly low, expected rain to fall and wind to blow.

10 Complete part of the lyrics "Rock Steady", by No Doubt.

[...]

____

It's a delicate environment

Retire but sleeping is a Shanti love

Be careful now don't wake it up

It's never gonna last

It's never gonna make it back alive

So how can we relax

I really hope that we will actually survive.

[...]

Extracted from <http://www.elyrics.net/read/n/no-doubt-lyrics/rock-steady-lyrics.html>. Accessed on February 26, 2010.

a ( ) Ready now, stop rocking it

b ( ) Silence now, stop talking

c (X) Steady now, stop rocking it

d ( ) Stop now, stop talking

e ( ) Rock now, stop rocking it

Refletindo sobre sua aprendizagem

Ao final desta unidade, você já é capaz de:

- Expressar pontos de vista em relação à ética e à moral e discutir com os colegas da sala e com o professor diversas atitudes das pessoas no cotidiano. ☑
- Identificar sinônimos para algumas palavras/expressões relacionadas ao tema do texto. ☐
- Relacionar novas palavras às suas definições. ☑
- Reconhecer o emprego e a função comunicativa de algumas *linking words*. ☐
- Reconhecer o emprego e a função comunicativa de *if clauses* (*zero, first,* e *second conditionals*). ☑
- Reescrever situações que apresentam dilemas típicos da adolescência usando *if clauses*. ☑
- Refletir sobre suas atitudes diante de situações que não são prováveis de acontecer. ☑
- Reconhecer características específicas de uma fábula. ☑

Aprimorando sua aprendizagem

- Peça ajuda ao professor ou aos colegas para que esclareçam suas dúvidas.
- Refaça os exercícios.
- Visite a biblioteca da sua escola ou uma biblioteca pública e consulte livros de gramática e/ou faça leituras de seu interesse.
- Assista a filmes em inglês.

2 Coping with Stress

PRE-READING

Look at the picture. What's going on with the zebra?

ILLUSTRATION: MILTON RODRIGUES ALVES

ART: RAFAEL GENTILE

File Edit View Favorites Tools Help

Address http://helpguide.org/mental/stress_signs.htm

What Is Stress?

Stress is a normal physical response to events that make you feel threatened or that upset your balance in some way. When you sense danger – whether it's real or imagined – the body's defenses kick into high gear in a rapid, automatic process known as the "fight-or-flight" reaction, or the *stress response*.

The stress response is the body's way of protecting you. When working properly, it helps you stay focused, energetic, and alert. In emergency situations, stress can save your life – giving you extra strength to defend yourself, for example, or spurring you to slam on the brakes to avoid an accident.

The stress response also helps you rise to meet challenges. Stress is what keeps you on your toes during a presentation at work, sharpens your concentration when you're attempting the game-winning free throw, or drives you to study for an exam when you'd rather be watching TV.

But beyond a certain point, stress stops being helpful and starts causing major damage to your health, your mood, your productivity, your relationships, and your quality of life.

Start

Extracted from <http://helpguide.org/mental/stress_signs.htm>. Accessed on January 20, 2010.

beyond a certain point: além de um certo ponto

free throw: lance livre

game-winning: vitorioso

sense: percebe

sharpens: afia

slam on the brakes: pisar nos freios

After Reading

1 Write T (true) or F (false).

a ( ) Stress can help you stay connected in your activities.

b ( ) Stress is always positive for the human body.

c ( ) Stress can help you to be strong for self defense.

2 Choose the best synonym for the words in bold.

2.1 "[...] the body's defenses **kick into high gear** in a rapid, automatic process [...]"

a ( ) slow down b ( ) elevate c ( ) stabilize

2.2 "Stress is what **keeps you on your toes** during a presentation at work [...]"

a ( ) makes you alert b ( ) destroys you c ( ) blinds you

2.3 "[...] or **spurring** you to slam on the brakes to avoid an accident."

a ( ) preventing b ( ) discouraging c ( ) encouraging

Appendix 2 page 152

3 Leia o extrato de texto abaixo e discuta-o com seus colegas.

RAFAEL GENTILE

Presença de *stress* na adolescência: quais as influências?

[...]

O que a presença de *stress* pode influenciar no adolescente? Muitas situações. Todos nós ficaríamos extremamente entediados se nada de diferente ou desafiador jamais acontecesse em nossas vidas, não é verdade? Entretanto, qualquer mudança significativa deve ser equilibrada com nossa habilidade de lidar com ela, assim como com o momento em que ela ocorra. Muitas mudanças ao mesmo tempo e ocorridas muito rapidamente podem frequentemente ser uma grande causa de *stress*.

O *stress* pode ser desencadeado por situações consideradas prazerosas, como se casar, ganhar dinheiro, passar no vestibular, etc., assim como por situações desagradáveis, como perder o emprego, não passar no vestibular, sofrer um acidente, doença ou morte de um membro da família, amigo, colega, divórcio/separação conjugal dos pais, mudança de casa. Como o adolescente passa por mudanças biológicas, sociais e psicológicas, ele pode ser afetado por *stress*. Essas situações possuem uma tendência de serem particularmente estressantes quando são imprevisíveis, inevitáveis, intensas, desconhecidas, significativas e sem escape.

[...]

Extraído de <http://www.crp13.org.br/one_news.asp?IDNews=455>.
Acessado em 25 de janeiro de 2010.

a Alguma vez você já esteve diante de uma situação causadora de grande estresse? Como lidou com ela?

b Você já tomou uma atitude em algum momento de estresse da qual se arrependeu? Como você contornou o problema?

c Como você reage às situações que lhe causam estresse?

Vocabulary in Use

1 Find in the text on page 22 the corresponding noun for the adjective **strong**. ______________

2 Match adjectives to nouns.

a	long	( )	width
b	wide	( )	breadth
c	deep	( )	youth
d	broad	( )	length
e	young	( )	depth

3 Complete the sentences using words from exercises 1 and 2.

a If you experience ______________ periods of stress, you can have serious health problems.

b ______________ is a period of life in which people don't feel a lot of stress: everything is nice and beautiful.

c Stress can give you extra ______________ to defend yourself in emergency situations.

d Do you know how ______________ this river is?

e He is a man with ______________ shoulders.

4 Write the words below in the appropriate column. Then translate them in the space provided.

drought dry strength strong true
truth warm warmth wide width

NOUNS	TRANSLATION	ADJECTIVES	TRANSLATION

5 Choose three adjectives from the exercises on page 24 and make true sentences about you, your friends, or your family members.

lucAs is the strenGth Guy who I Knew

Vitor is the only one who Know the truth

boinG 777 is the width AIRCRAft in the MARket

Grammar in Use

CONDITIONAL SENTENCES (IF CLAUSES)

Third Conditional

Utilizado para expressar uma ação que não se concretizou no passado e sua provável consequência.	If the students **had taken** some time off, (Past Perfect) they **would have been** better prepared to (would have + Past Participle) start another school year.

Nota

Verbos modais (*can*, *may*, *might* e *could*) também podem ser usados nas três frases condicionais.	If I **have** time, I **can** / **may help** you with the housework. If I **had** R$ 300,00, I **might buy** a new bike. If Joseph **had run faster**, he **could have won** the competition.

1 Match.

a If they had driven more carefully, ...
b If Susie had saved money, ...
c If I had listened to your advice, ...
d If you hadn't shouted, ...
e If we had had leisure time, ...
f If he hadn't married Susie, ...

(A) the accident wouldn't have happened.
(d) nobody would have come to rescue you.
(f) he would have chosen Liz.
(b) she would have bought her own house.
(e) we would have had more fun.
(c) I wouldn't have gone out in the rain.

2 Rewrite the sentences to comment on what probably would or wouldn't have happened. The first one is done for you.

a If they saw the robber, they would call the police.
If they had seen the robber, they would have called the police.

b If you were present, things wouldn't be different.
If you had present, things would have be different

c If we lived there, I would go to the beach more often.
If we had lived there, I wouldn't go to the beach more often

d If Stella did business in a foreign country, she would get more money.
If Stella had business in a foreign country, she wouldn't get more money

e If my doctor made a mistake like that, he wouldn't admit it.
If my doctor has made a mistake like that, he would admit it

3 Choose the correct verb form.

3.1 I ________ more often if I lived near the gym.

- **a** (X) will work out
- **b** (   ) would work out

3.2 They ________ earlier if you say it's necessary.

- **a** (X) may arrive
- **b** (   ) had arrived

3.3 ________ for advice if you don't know what to do.

- **a** (   ) Ask
- **b** (X) Will ask

3.4 If Sam had left me a message, I ________ the cafeteria.

- **a** (   ) would leave
- **b** (X) wouldn't have left

3.5 If Patricia meets her boyfriend's boss, she ________ him for a raise.

- **a** (   ) would have begged
- **b** (X) will beg

3.6 If you ________ your glasses, the teacher would have asked you to read the text out loud.

- **a** (X) hadn't forgotten
- **b** (   ) would forget

4 Complete the sentences using the phrases in the boxes. Make the necessary changes.

have time	**be rich**
be better off	**see the TV news**
grab	**not buy it**
study more	**let you know**
wave	**faint**

a If you don't need the product, you wouldn't buy it.

b They wouldn't sell their apartment if they be rich.

c Chris will visit her grandma if she study more.

d If I have time, I would travel around the world.

e If we had stayed up late, we see the tv news.

f If he be better off, he would have passed the tests.

g I let know if I had seen you.

h If I decide to go to Sam's birthday party, I let you know.

i My sister faint if she came across her favorite actor.

j If Max didn't have lunch, he grab a sandwich.

5 Answer the questions below with complete sentences.

a If your house were on fire, what would you save first?

if my house were on fire, I will save my recharger cellphone

b If someone knocked on the door of your house in the middle of the night, would you open the door immediately?

If someone knocked on the door of your house in the middle of the..., I will

c If the weather had been better, what would you have done?

if the weather had been better, I would have done

6 Your best friend is not a very tidy or organized person, so you decide to give him or her some advice. Match the columns. Then identify the pictures that represent each situation.

A	B
a If you put on clean clothes, ...	( ) you would find out what was going on in the world.
b If you had gone to bed earlier during the week, ...	( ) you wouldn't have failed all the finals.
c If you sometimes read the newspaper or watched the news on TV, ...	( ) you will look more stylish.
d If you turn the radio down, ...	( ) you will hear what I am saying.
e If you had at least listened to your teachers in class, ...	( ) you wouldn't have felt so tired in the mornings.

ILLUSTRATIONS: VICENTE MENDONÇA

7 Choose the best meaning for the sentences below.

7.1 If Daniel had a girlfriend, he would be happier.

a ( ) Daniel is unhappy with his girlfriend.

b (X) Daniel doesn't have a girlfriend.

c ( ) Daniel has a lousy girlfriend.

7.2 If you are in trouble, get in touch with me.

a ( ) In case of trouble, I will call my boss.

b ( ) No matter what happens, don't get in touch with me.

c (X) You should call me if you are in trouble.

7.3 If I had gone to the club, I would have given you a lift.

a (X) I didn't go to the club.

b ( ) I went to the club.

c ( ) I didn't get a lift when I went to the club.

7.4 If he had climbed the mountain, he would have hurt himself.

a ( ) He hurt himself.

b ( ) He climbed the mountain.

c (X) He didn't climb the mountain.

7.5 If it rains, we won't go jogging.

a ( ) We will go jogging anyway.

b (X) Depending on the weather, we won't go jogging.

c ( ) We can't go jogging.

7.6 If Ted read more books, he would improve his writing skills.

a (X) Ted doesn't read books.

b ( ) Ted loves reading.

c ( ) Ted didn't read last semester.

7.7 If Barbara had had more time, she would have helped with the housework.

a ( ) Barbara had some time off, but she didn't help with the housework.

b ( ) Barbara helped with the housework because she had time.

c (X) Barbara didn't help with the housework because she didn't have time.

7.8 If I knew you would need these numbers, I would program the computer to calculate them.

a ( ) He programmed the computer because he knew his boss needed those numbers.

b (X) He didn't program the computer because he didn't know his boss needed those numbers.

c ( ) He didn't program the computer even though he knew his boss needed those numbers.

Reading

File Edit View Favorites Tools Help

Address http://www.lifespan.org/services/childhealth/parenting/teen-stress.htm Go Links »

Helping Teens Cope with Stress

by Jennifer Dyl, PhD
Bradley Hospital psychologist

Seventeen-year-old Marissa is juggling many roles. She has a demanding part-time job, plays two varsity sports, is studying for the SATs, and is trying to decide where to go to college and how to pay for it. She also has a term paper and an Internet project due this week, needs to find a date and a dress for the prom, is worried that she has gained five pounds, and is afraid that her best friend is mad at her. While Marissa used to feel confident and excited by life's challenges, she has recently been feeling overwhelmed, out of control and "stressed out."

Marissa's story is typical of the daily pressures teens face.

"Stress" is defined as the way our bodies and minds react to life changes. Since adolescence is a period of significant change – including physical, emotional, social, and academic changes – many teens are under more stress than at any other time of life.

Teenage Stress Factors

- Academic pressure and career decisions
- Pressure to wear certain types of clothing or hairstyles
- Pressure to try drugs, alcohol, or sex
- Pressure to fit in with peer groups and measure up to others
- Adaptation to bodily changes
- Family and peer conflicts
- Taking on too many activities at one time

It is very important for teens to learn to handle stress, as long-term build-up of stress that is not handled effectively may lead to problems, including physical illness, anxiety, or depression – which call for professional help.

[...]

Start

Extracted from <http://www.lifespan.org/services/childhealth/parenting/teen-stress.htm>. Accessed on January 21, 2010.

cope with: enfrentar, lidar com

juggling: assumindo (ao mesmo tempo)

long-term build-up of stress: longo acúmulo de estresse

measure up to: ser bom o suficiente

overwhelmed: sobrecarregada

peer groups: grupos de pessoas da mesma idade e com hábitos semelhantes

prom: baile de formatura de estudantes

roles: papéis, funções

SATs: (Scholastic Assessment Test) – exames para entrar na universidade

varsity sports: atividades esportivas com as equipes da escola.

After Reading

1 Check the statements which are true according to the text.

a (T) Most teens go through the same problems Marissa is facing.

b (F) Life changes are the leading cause of stress.

c (F) The family is the only non-stress element in one's life.

d (F) Teenagers tend to be independent and not to care about other people's opinions.

e (T) If not handled appropriately, stress can lead to serious problems.

f (T) Having periods of doing nothing at all helps to combat stress.

2 Correct the wrong information in the sentences below. Refer to the text on page 30.

a Marissa is not interested in going to university because she can't afford it.

Marissa has the interest in going to the university, thus she is thinking how to pay for it

b Nowadays, Marissa is relaxed and her emotions are under control.

Marissa is "overwhelmed" with the amount of duties and stress that she is going through!!

c There are unknown problems caused by stress.

There are many known problems related to stress anxiety, depression and stress

d Childhood and adolescence are periods of significant changes.

3 Read the dictionary entry and do the activity.

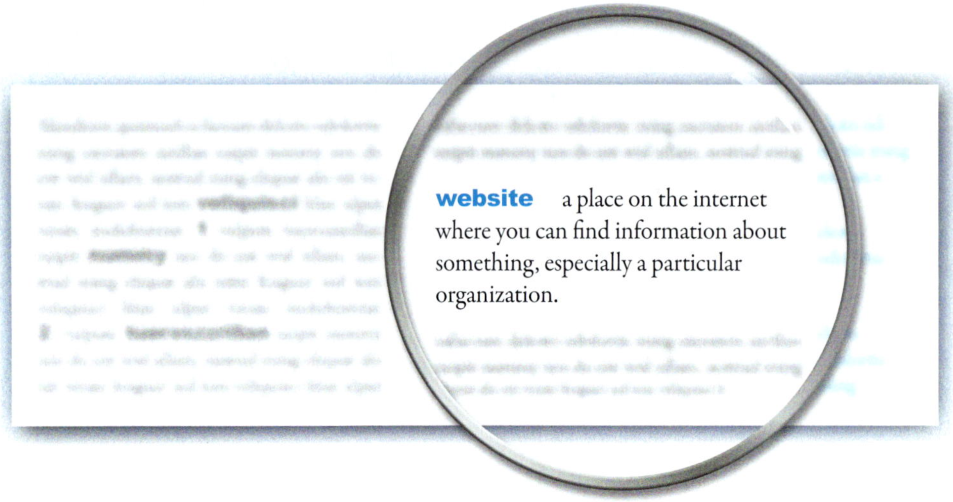

ANDREZA MOREIRA

Longman Dictionary of Contemporary English. London: Longman, 2003. 4. ed. p. 1870.

Assinale as principais características encontradas nos textos das páginas 22 e 30.

	Texto 1 (p. 22)	Texto 2 (p. 30)
Uso de imagens	X	X
Manchetes atraentes	X	X
Opinião pessoal do autor	X	
Anúncios de publicidade		
Presença de logotipos		
Link de contato	X	X
Links para outras informações		
Opções para outros idiomas		

RAFAEL GENTILE

Consultando outras fontes

filme: *Tratamento de choque* (EUA, 2003; direção: Peter Segal)

livro: *Pega leve! Enfrentando o estresse da adolescência* (Artes e Ofícios; autora: Ana Maria Rossi)

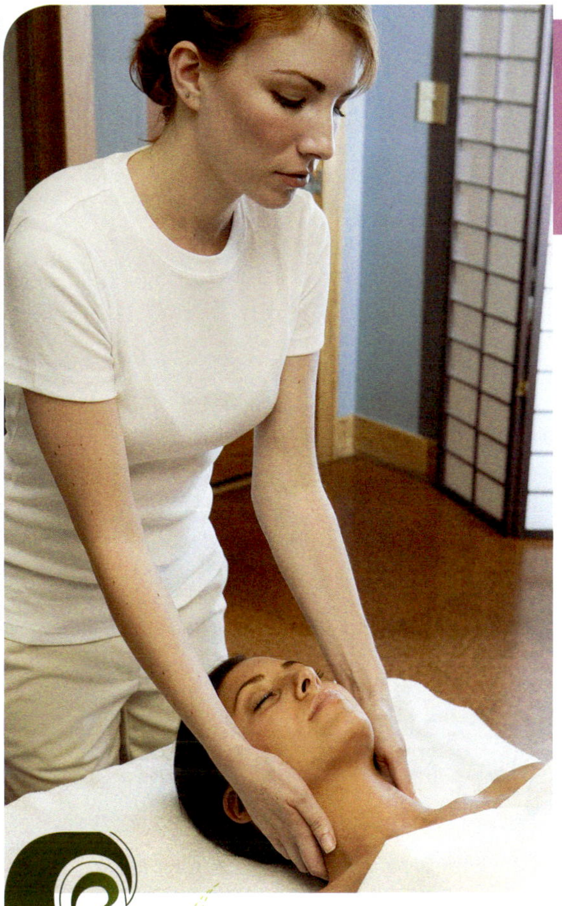

PHOTO: ONFOCUS / SHUTTERSTOCK; JUPITER UNLIMITED / IMAGEPLUS; ART: RAFAEL GENTILE

Massage Therapist

There are many ways in which a person can unwind or cool down when he or she is stressed or tired — and one of them is to get a good massage. Not everybody is entitled to give you a massage, but a massage therapist is.

Massage therapists perform different kinds of massotherapy and reflexology maneuvers to relieve clients' pain and to help clients relax. Before choosing the techniques to be used, massage therapists should bear in mind the specific needs of each client. That's why clients have to be honest when talking to the therapists before starting their treatments.

Massage therapists work in hospitals, fitness centers, spas, shopping malls, physical therapy centers, nursing homes, sports clubs, hotels, sports medicine centers, beauty parlors, and even in private offices as self-employed workers.

In order to become a massage therapist, one has to take a 1200- to 1320-hour course, depending on the school. The good news is that you can take this vocational course at the same time as high school.

Based on <http://www.bls.gov/oco/ocos295.htm>; <http://online.onetcenter.org/link/summary/31-9011.00>; <http://www.careerplanner.com/Job-Descriptions/Massage-Therapists.cfm>. Accessed on February 23, 2010.

bear in mind: ter em mente
cool down: acalmar-se
maneuvers: manobras
relieve: aliviar
unwind: relaxar

Você gostaria de ser técnico em massoterapia? Por quê? / Por que não?

Additional Practice

For exercises 1 to 10, choose the best alternative.

1 "Passepartout remained on deck as long as the tempest lasted, being unable to remain quiet below, and taking it into his head to aid the progress of the ship by lending a hand with the crew. He ________ the captain, officers, and sailors, who could not help laughing at his impatience, with all sorts of questions. He wanted to know exactly how long the storm was going to last; whereupon he was referred to the barometer, which seemed to have no intention of rising."

Extracted from *Around the World in Eighty Days*, by Jules Verne. Dover Publications, Inc. – Unabridged republication of the 1873 translation by George Makepeace Towle of Jules Verne's *Le Tour du Monde en Quatre-vingts Jours* – 2000. p. 76.

a ( ) strength
b ( ) overwhelmed
c ( ) threatened
d ( ) spurring
e ( ) sharpen

2 "The health of youngsters in China is being ________ by the stress they come up against at school, it has been discovered."

Extracted from <http://www.vsointernational.org/news/19570967/chinese-childrens-health-threatened-by-stress-at-school>. Accessed on January 21, 2010.

a ( ) strength
b ( ) threatened
c ( ) spurred
d ( ) spurring
e ( ) sharpen

3 You need to learn how to transform stress into ________ so that you can deal with pressure without risking your health.

a ( ) strength
b ( ) threatened
c ( ) overwhelmed
d ( ) spurring
e ( ) sharpen

4 My grandmother has Alzheimer's disease. The doctor said that memory loss may ________ stress. That explains why she gets angry sometimes.

a ( ) spur
b ( ) gear
c ( ) sharpen
d ( ) slam
e ( ) overwhelm

5 ________ sports demand a lot of dedication and commitment. They also offer athletes the opportunity to compete at a higher level, which sometimes increases the athletes' stress levels.

a ( ) Gear
b ( ) Strength
c ( ) Sharpen
d ( ) Varsity
e ( ) Slam

6 My career would have been better by now if...

a ( ) stress didn't cause me to make some really bad choices in the past.
b ( ) stress caused me to make some really bad choices in the past.
c ( ) stress hadn't caused me to make some really bad choices in the past.
d ( ) stress will cause me to make some really bad choices in the past.
e ( ) stress causes me to make some really bad choices in the past.

7 Kate hasn't been herself lately. I know her well and she...

a ( ) wouldn't be stressed unless something very serious happened.
b ( ) wouldn't have been stressed unless something very serious happened.
c ( ) will not be stressed unless something very serious happened.

d ( ) is stressed unless something very serious happens.

e ( ) wouldn't be stressed unless something very serious didn't happen.

8 **Carol:** So, how was your doctor's appointment this morning?

Laura: Awful! I didn't like the new doctor at the clinic. I've been going to Dr. Stevenson for 27 years! And I ________

a ( ) will schedule an appointment with him if he moved to another country!

b ( ) would schedule an appointment with him if he moves to another country!

c ( ) would have scheduled an appointment with him if he hadn't moved to another country!

d ( ) schedule an appointment with him if he moved to another country!

e ( ) would have scheduled an appointment with him if he moves to another country!

9 **Sarah:** Larry called me last night to apologize for the weekend.

Cindy: ________

a ( ) Why does he apologize if he doesn't do anything wrong?

b ( ) Why did he apologize if he did anything wrong?

c ( ) Why hadn't he apologized if he didn't do anything wrong?

d ( ) Why doesn't he apologize if doesn't do anything wrong?

e ( ) Why did he apologize if he didn't do anything wrong?

10 Do you know the tale of the hare and the tortoise? If the hare ________ a nap, he would have won the race against the tortoise!

a ( ) took

b ( ) didn't take

c ( ) hadn't taken

d ( ) takes

e ( ) will take

Refletindo sobre sua aprendizagem

Ao final desta unidade, você já é capaz de:

- Fazer leitura de imagens e relacioná-las ao texto verbal. ☐
- Localizar informações específicas no texto, analisá-las e corrigi-las, se necessário. ☐
- Identificar sinônimos para algumas palavras/expressões relacionadas ao tema do texto. ☐
- Expressar pontos de vista em relação às influências do estresse na vida do adolescente, discutir com os colegas da sala e com o professor as causas do estresse e o que pode ser feito para lidar com situações que geram estresse. ☐
- Reconhecer e diferenciar substantivos e adjetivos. ☐
- Identificar o emprego e a função comunicativa de *if clauses* (*third conditionals*). ☐
- Identificar e aplicar os quatro tipos de *if clauses* estudados. ☐
- Refletir sobre suas atitudes diante de situações que apresentam todos os tipos de *if clauses* estudados.
- Reconhecer características específicas de *websites*. ☐

Aprimorando sua aprendizagem

- Peça ajuda ao professor ou aos colegas para que esclareçam suas dúvidas.
- Refaça os exercícios.
- Visite a biblioteca da sua escola ou uma biblioteca pública e consulte livros de gramática e/ou faça leituras de seu interesse.
- Assista a filmes em inglês.

Language in Action 1

1 What stresses you out? Do this quiz and see what kind of person you are. Use the code given.

VICENTE MENDONÇA

1 = never | 2 = sometimes | 3 = usually | 4 = always

- [2] I get angry when I have to wait in line for more than 10 minutes.
- [1] It's not easy for me to relax.
- [2] I become irritated when people speak slowly.
- [3] I enjoy being under pressure no matter who is pressing me.
- [1] I get bored if I stay alone in silence.
- [2] I feel excited if I am under pressure.
- [3] I always do things in a hurry, even when I don't need to.
- [1] I am not patient to listen to people.
- [4] I keep busy all the time on weekends.
- [1] I interrupt people when they are talking if I need to talk to them.

Now add up your score.

10-20	You don't worry about life at all.
21-30	You know how to relax, but sometimes you take certain things seriously.
31-40	You need to change your behavior immediately. Your level of stress is high!

Do you agree with the score you got? Why? / Why not?

Yes. I Agreo Sometimes I get mad

2 Below you will find different ways of managing stress. Which of them do you think are good ideas? What do you do when you feel stressed? Talk to a classmate.

VICENTE MENDONÇA

Do exercise.	Go out with friends.
Watch TV.	Listen to relaxing music.
Eat more slowly.	Sleep long hours.
Talk to somebody in your family.	Eat a bar of chocolate.

3 (2) Listen to three people talking about what stresses them and what they do when they feel stressed. Take notes.

Susan

Owen

David

Writing

Go back to the quiz on page 36. Write three more questions. Use some of the adjectives listed below.

angry bored busy calm energetic excited frightened impatient
irritated nervous patient relaxed stressed worried

Do you get irritated when your father argue you?

Are you considarated a patient person?

How many times you scream per week?

3 The Battle for Equality

PRE-READING

Look at the photo. Can you guess what this woman is doing? What's the relation between the photo and the text?

Monday, Jan. 11, 2010

The Change We Need

By Cherie Blair

When I was a child, we had to live in our grandmother's house. My mother, a lone parent, couldn't get a mortgage simply because she was a woman, even though she had a well-paid job. When I qualified as a lawyer in the UK three decades ago, women in the legal profession still had to overcome open prejudice and discrimination. So when we examine the position of women across the Middle East, it's important not to despair – or forget our own past.

In fact, when I chat with women in the region, I can tell them from personal experience that life does change and that once progress starts, it can develop much more quickly than they might expect. No one would claim, of course, that the position of women in the Middle East in general is one that inspires confidence. But across the region – and often defying Western preconceptions – the battle for equality is making gains.

Few would guess, for example, that the states with the world's highest ratio of women to men in higher education are in the gulf. In Kuwait, women were elected to parliament for the first time this year. And women have been appointed to important ministerial posts in neighboring countries; Jordan has four women in its Cabinet, including Hala Latouf, the Minister for

Dr. Saleha Mahmood Abedin, professor of Sociology from Pakistan

Social Development. There are women judges, too, in Palestine, Bahrain, and the United Arab Emirates – something that would have been hard to imagine a generation ago. And women are taking an increasingly prominent role in the economy; in the West Bank recently I met female lawyers, architects, and even a lift engineer. Of course, we can't get carried away. In some Middle Eastern countries, the progress of women can appear desperately slow. And in none have women attained anything like the opportunities we take for granted in Western Europe or North America. Women still have to contend daily with male-dominated societies and culture, often underpinned by discriminatory laws. They may have more opportunities to study, but even well-educated women struggle to find jobs – and when they do, career progression is difficult. The expectations that men stay in control and women at home remain strong.

[...]

Extracted from <http://www.time.com/time/printout/0,8816,1950674,00.html>. Accessed on January 14, 2010.

PHOTO: OMAR / AFP PHOTO / GETTY IMAGES; ART: RAFAEL GENTILE

attained: conseguiram; realizaram
claim: alegar, afirmar
contend: combater
defying: desafiando
despair: desanimar
overcome: superar
ratio: proporção
take for granted: presumimos
underpinned: sustentadas

After Reading

1 Check the alternatives that are correct according to the text.

a (T) The author has been a lawyer since 1980.
b (T) The educational position of women across the Middle East hasn't changed at all.
c (F) Men still dominate society and culture and they are expected to be in control.

2 Find parts of the text that mean the same as the Portuguese sections below.

a "[...] mesmo tendo um trabalho bem pago."

"Women in legal profession"
____

b "[...] mulheres estão assumindo um papel cada vez mais notável na economia."

"In none have women attained anything like the opportunities
____

c "[...] nós não podemos nos deixar levar pelas circunstâncias."

____

3 Where can we find a text like the one on page 38?

a ( ) In a recipe book.
b ( ) In a teen magazine.
c (X) In a newspaper or blog.
d ( ) In a tour brochure.

4 Leia os textos abaixo e discuta-os com seus colegas.

"Enquanto o homem e a mulher não se reconhecerem como semelhantes, enquanto não se respeitarem como pessoas em que, do ponto de vista social, político e econômico, não há a menor diferença, os seres humanos estarão condenados a não verem o que têm de melhor: a sua liberdade."

Simone de Beauvoir

"Na sociedade moderna, a mulher está cada vez mais conquistando seu espaço no ambiente profissional e participando das mudanças ocorridas na contemporaneidade. Aos poucos as habilidades e características femininas começam a ser valorizadas pela sociedade, deixando a mulher, aos poucos, de ser uma mera coadjuvante em determinados segmentos sociais e profissionais, possibilitando cada vez mais o seu acesso às posições estratégicas em suas profissões."

RAFAEL GENTILE

Extraído de <http://afinsophia.wordpress.com/2009/03/07/o-papel-da-mulher-na-sociedade-moderna>. Acessado em 26 de janeiro de 2010.

a Você acha que a mulher deve participar ativamente da estrutura social?
b As mulheres de sua família trabalham fora? Que tipo de cargo elas ocupam?
c Você concorda com a opinião de Simone de Beauvoir? Justifique sua resposta.
d Quais foram as conquistas sociais femininas no mercado de trabalho ao longo das últimas décadas do século XX?

Vocabulary in Use

1 In the sentence "My mother, a lone **parent**, couldn't get a mortgage simply because she was a woman, even though she had a well-paid job." The word "parent" is a false cognate. What does it mean? ____________________

2 Choose the correct translation for the false cognate underlined in each sentence below. Use the words in the box. Some words will not be used.

> **TIP**
> Um **falso cognato** geralmente vem do latim e tem semelhança com uma palavra em língua portuguesa, mas seu sentido é diferente.

fábrica	biblioteca	empurre	legenda	puxe	maior
fantasias	lenda	prefeito	livraria	parentes	

a Yesterday Dora studied at the <u>library</u>. ____________________

b The <u>mayor</u> of the city promised water treatment and new bridges. ____________________

c <u>Push</u> the door to open it. ____________________

d He was a <u>legend</u> in his town. ____________________

e Kids wore scary <u>costumes</u> at the Halloween party. ____________________

f All our <u>relatives</u> will come to my daughter's fifteenth birthday in April.
____

3 Complete the sentences below with the appropriate words from the box.

attend	educated	journal	lunch
actually	beef	pretended	

a *CALL* is a famous ____________________ in Applied Linguistics. It offers articles about learning online and computer use in education.

b My parents and I have ____________________ at home at about noon.

c Women may have more opportunities to study, but even well-____________________ ones struggle to find jobs.

d She is not a regular student. She doesn't ____________________ classes regularly.

e Vegetarians don't eat ____________________ or other kinds of meat.

f He ____________________ to understand, in order not to appear ignorant.

g **A:** Did you get a good grade on the final test?

B: Yes, ____________________, it was the best one I got.

Appendix 3
page 153

Grammar in Use

DIRECT AND INDIRECT SPEECH (I)

Para relatar o que uma pessoa disse, usamos o discurso direto ou o discurso indireto:	
Direct speech: reproduz exatamente o que foi dito pela pessoa. Aspas são usadas.	The teacher said, "We are going to have a test tomorrow."
Indirect speech: conta o que foi dito, usando nossas palavras. Aspas não são usadas e o uso de *that* é opcional.	The teacher said (that) we / they were going to have a test the next day.

Para usarmos o discurso indireto, fazemos algumas modificações nas frases. Observe:

Direct Speech	Indirect Speech
He said, "I **need** to work late **today**." (Simple Present)	He said (that) he **needed** to work late **that day**. (Simple Past)
He said, "I **met** Sue **yesterday**." (Simple Past)	He said (that) he **had met** Sue **the day before**. (Past Perfect)
She said, "I **will** go shopping **tomorrow**." (will)	She said (that) she **would** go shopping **the next day**. (would)
She said, "I **am studying** now." (Present Continuous)	She said (that) she **was studying then**. (Past Continuous)
They said, "We **were eating** 5 minutes ago." (Past Continuous)	They said (that) they **had been eating** 5 minutes **before**. (Past Perfect Continuous)
They said, "We **have finished our** task." (Present Perfect)	They said (that) they **had finished their** task. (Past Perfect)
She said, "I **have been studying** English for seven years." (Present Perfect Continuous)	She said she **had been studying** English for seven years. (Past Perfect Continuous)
Mark said, "We **had gone** there before." (Past Perfect)	Mark said (that) they **had gone** there before. (Past Perfect)

Com *modal verbs*, também temos algumas mudanças:	
Direct Speech	**Indirect Speech**
I said, "I **can** arrange **this** party."	I said (that) I **could** arrange **that** party.
He said, "I **must** have a computer to do **my** job."	He said (that) he **had to** have a computer to do **his** job.
She said, "I **may** open the window."	She said (that) she **might** open the window.

Notas

Quando o verbo da oração do *direct speech* estiver no *Simple Present, Future* ou *Present Perfect*, não há mudança obrigatória no tempo verbal da oração no *indirect speech*.	He says, "I **live** in the suburbs." He says (that) he **lives** in the suburbs.

1 Choose the correct alternative.

a The teacher said, "I'm not coming tomorrow."

(X) The teacher said he/she was not coming the following day.

(   ) The teacher said he/she is not coming the following day.

b Sue's mother said, "You should take an umbrella."

(   ) Sue's mother told her not to take an umbrella.

(X) Sue's mother told her to take an umbrella.

c Jim said, "I'll go to the movie theater on Sunday."

(   ) Jim said he was going to the movie theater on Sunday.

(X) Jim said he would go to the movie theater on Sunday.

d "Don't turn the TV on."

(   ) He didn't tell me to turn the TV on.

(X) He told me not to turn the TV on.

e My sister said to me, "I start a diet every Monday."

(X) My sister told me she starts a diet every Monday.

(   ) My sister said me she starts a diet every Monday.

f Brenda said to me, "I have asked my sister to come with me."

(X) Brenda told me she had asked her sister to go with her.

(   ) Brenda told me she has asked her sister to go with her.

TIP

Jim said, "I have to study today."

Jim said (that) he had to study that day.

Jim said, "Mom, I have to study today."

Jim told his mom he had to study that day.

g John's father said, "I sent you a message this morning."

( ) John's father said he has sent him a message that morning.

(X) John's father said he had sent him a message that morning.

h The kids said, "We were playing in the yard, Mom."

( ) The kids told their mom they are playing in the yard.

(X) The kids told their mom they were playing in the yard.

2 Match the indirect and direct speech.

1 The weatherman said we would have heavy rain in the South.

2 I told her I really liked her project.

3 She said she would go to the bank later.

4 She said the kids had studied hard.

5 She said she couldn't do that at that moment because she had a lot of work to finish.

6 Lisa said she would wash Mike's car and he could cook dinner.

(5) "I can't do this now. I have a lot of work to finish."

(2) "I really like your project."

(3) "I'll go to the bank later."

(6) "I'll wash your car and you can cook dinner."

(4) "The kids have studied hard."

(1) "We'll have heavy rain in the South."

3 Complete the sentences. Use the phrases in the box.

he hadn't finished his Biology project yet
my sister had gone to the movies with them
she has been tired lately
they hadn't traveled to Mexico
we had bought a new TV set for mom

a Joe said that he hadn't finished his biology project yet.

b Sophie says that she has been tired lately.

c Louis and Jamie said that we had bought a new tv set for mom.

d Thomas and I said that they hadn't traveled to mexico.

e My parents said that My sister had gone to the movies with them

4 Unscramble the words to form sentences.

a me / that / Chris / told / she / sick / was

She told me that, Chris was sick

b Bill / he / said / travel / would / the next day / that

He said that, Bill would travel the next day

c Ann / told / her husband / take / should / a nap / he

Ann told her husband, he should take a nap

d teacher / said / he / would / my / be / Mr. Lawson / that / new

Mr. Lawson said that he would be my new teacher

5 Rewrite the sentences using indirect speech.

a I said, "We have to concentrate to do these exercises."

I said, we has to concentrate to do there exercises

b The girl said, "My mom can't pick me up at school today."

the girl said, my mom couldn't pick me up at school today

c They said, "We were planning to move out."

they said, we was planning to move out

d He said, "I have been studying a lot."

He said, I here been studying a lot

e We said, "You will call for help."

We said, you would call for help

f They said, "We don't have enough information to judge the case."

they said, we didn't has enough information to judge the case

6 Read the cartoons on page 45. Make the necessary changes to transform them into indirect speech.

a The little girl said that her birthday is in the saturday.

b Santa said his sure that they will enjoy their presents.

c The teacher said that my ... will help tomorrow.

d Jenny said glad to came to garage sale.

e The secretary said would be in shortly.

f The woman said there skirts are on sale.

A

Saturday's my birthday.

B

I'm sure Laura and Tony will enjoy their presents.

C

Mindy, I'm going to need your help tomorrow.

D

I'm so glad we came to this garage sale.

E

Mr. Jackson will be in shortly.

F

These skirts are on sale.

Reading

PHOTO: CHRISTOPHER VAN SCHAIK / SHUTTERSTOCK; ART: RAFAEL GENTILE

Lei Maria da Penha

The *"Lei Maria da Penha"* (Lei 11.340 / 2006) was signed into law by the Brazilian president Luiz Inácio Lula da Silva on August 7, 2006. The law was named after Maria da Penha Maia Fernandes, as a symbolic reparation and recognition for this woman's twenty-year battle to bring her case to justice. In 1983, Maria da Penha almost lost her life twice at the hands of her husband, Marco Antonio Heredia Viveiros. Maria da Penha became paraplegic as a result of the abuse, and her story gained international attention. The feminist and women's movement in Brazil had, of course, a crucial role in the process of elaboration and passing of the *"Lei Maria da Penha"*. While it is perhaps too soon to measure the real impact of this legislation in reducing domestic violence in Brazil, its passage and formulation as an instrument of social, political, judicial, and cultural change is deserving of notice. The *"Lei Maria da Penha"* shares the perspective that domestic violence is a violation of the human rights of women and stipulates a national, integrated set of public policies to eradicate this grave problem. In this sense, the provisions of the law include the adoption and enhancement of preventive, punitive, protective, as well as assistance-related policies. The following documents provide information on the provisions of this law and shed light on the existing challenges to its successful implementation. They also equip advocates and activists with tools to better monitor and evaluate the public policies designed to eradicate domestic violence in Brazil.

Extracted from <http://new.vawnet.org/category/index_pages.php?category_id=784>. Accessed on February 4, 2010.

deserving of notice: digno de menção
passing: aprovação
policies: políticas
shed light on: esclarece

After Reading

1 Match the columns to form true statements about the article on page 46.

a The "*Lei Maria da Penha*" deals with...

b Violence against women is still...

c The effect of the "*Lei Maria da Penha*" in the reduction of domestic violence in Brazil...

d Domestic violence...

e The "*Lei Maria da Penha*"...

(b) a grave problem in Brazil.

(e) is not very clear.

(A) domestic violence.

(d) is a violation of the human rights of women.

(c) includes protective and assistance-related policies for women.

2 Choose synonyms from the box to substitute the underlined words. Use the glossary if necessary.

give disabled identification supervise put an end to calculate addition

a "[...] as a symbolic reparation and recognition for this woman's twenty-year battle to bring her case to justice."

Identification

b "Maria da Penha became paraplegic as a result of the abuse [...]."

disabled

c "While it is perhaps too soon to measure the real impact of this legislation in reducing domestic violence in Brazil [...]."

Calculate

d "The '*Lei Maria da Penha*' [...] stipulates a national, integrated set of public policies to eradicate this grave problem."

put an end to

e "In this sense, the provisions of the law include the adoption and enhancement of preventive, punitive, protective [...]."

addition

f "The following documents provide information [...]."

give

g "They also equip advocates and activists with tools to better monitor and evaluate the public policies [...]."

supervise

3 The texts on pages 38 and 46 are articles written for printed or digital publications. Decide if each text displays the characteristics below. Write (1) for *The Change We Need*, (2) for *Lei Maria da Penha* and (0) for neither.

a (1) Discusses topics and issues of contemporary life.

b (1) Is based on statistical or other evidence.

c (0) The author's opinions are clear and evident.

d (1) Reports the results of a study.

e (2) Makes an assessment of a certain situation from the point of view of the writer.

f (2) Displays the writer's name.

Consultando outras fontes

filmes: *Frida* (México/Canadá/EUA, 2002; direção: Julie Taymor)
Coco antes de Chanel (França, 2009; direção: Anne Fontaine)

livro: *Dicionário mulheres do Brasil* (Jorge Zahar Editor; organizadores: Schuma Schumaher e Érico Vital Brazil)

músicas: "Woman" (John Lennon)
"She" (Elvis Costello)

Journalist

Do you sometimes feel like making a difference in our society? Do you believe that information and awareness are the strongest weapons at our disposal to fight against whatever is wrong out there? If your answer is *yes*, then you should consider becoming a journalist.

Information is raw material for journalists. Once they learn about a situation or fact, they have to investigate the source, search for details, and sometimes even interview people to make sure that that situation or fact is true. Then they divulge all possible information, making it public to all recipients of the coverage, so that everybody can be aware of that situation or fact.

A journalist's job is to bring out the truth, no matter the subject. That is an important means of exerting power, for once a piece of news is broadcast, there's no way back. That's why a journalist must be extremely ethical and responsible. His or her commitment to society is directly related to his commitment to the truth. He or she must chase after the truth, wherever it is, before broadcasting his or her stories. A journalist must never divulge erroneous facts which might involve innocent people or institutions.

A journalist can work in any kind of media: radio, TV, magazines, internet, newspaper, or as a freelancer.

According to Brazilian laws, anybody can be a journalist, even those who haven't taken any specific course. But the industry still prefers graduated students those who are properly prepared for the seriousness of this profession. So, if you want to become a journalist, you should graduate from high school and then take a four-year college course.

PHOTO: SALIM OCTOBER / SHUTTERSTOCK; ART: RAFAEL GENTILE

at our disposal: de que dispomos, à nossa disposição
awareness: qualidade de ser ciente, atento
bring out: mostrar, fazer aparecer
broadcast: transmitida, emitida
chase after: perseguir; buscar
commitment: compromisso
exerting: exercendo
feel like: tem vontade de
raw material: matéria-prima

Você gostaria de ser jornalista? Por quê? / Por que não?

Additional Practice

For exercises 1 to 8, choose the best alternative.

1 "[...]

Participants in Tuesday's meeting included many ________ Egyptian politicians and intellectuals, such as coordinator of the Egyptian campaign against succession [...]."

Extracted from <http://latimesblogs.latimes.com/babylonbeyond/2010/02/egypt-elbaradei-forms-new-front-for-change.html>. Accessed on January 24, 2010.

a ( ) lone
b ( ) prejudice
c ( ) defying
d ( ) ratio
e ( ) prominent

2 There aren't many women working in the Congress. In fact, Mrs. Herrera is the ________ woman in this list I have here.

a ( ) lone
b ( ) prejudice
c ( ) defying
d ( ) ratio
e ( ) attained

3 Those blonde girls are ________ the stereotype by showing they are as intelligent as the other girls in the class.

a ( ) defying
b ( ) struggle
c ( ) passing
d ( ) contend
e ( ) lone

4 They were protesting against the abortion law. Some people got ________ with all of the excitement and broke some windows, but no one got really hurt.

a ( ) passing
b ( ) underpinned
c ( ) carried away
d ( ) contend
e ( ) eradicate

5 **Kathryn:** I met a girl from Iraq at the party last night.

Debra: Iraq? Wow, that's unusual. What's she doing here?

Kathryn: She came as a guest to speak at a conference about women's rights. Can you believe that in Iraq, women only ________ the right to vote and run for office in 1980?

a ( ) underpinned
b ( ) struggle
c ( ) contend
d ( ) attained
e ( ) passing

6 The new secretary has just quit. She said that our boss ________ an inappropriate comment about her clothes. She felt humiliated and cried for hours.

a ( ) makes
b ( ) had made
c ( ) made
d ( ) will make
e ( ) makes

7 Anita lived in a country where women are considered inferior. Although she enjoyed living there, she ________.

a ( ) said that women is treated with total disrespect.
b ( ) said that women can treated with total disrespect.
c ( ) said that women will be treated with total disrespect.
d ( ) said that women was treated with total disrespect.
e ( ) said that women were treated with total disrespect.

8 **Cindy:** I was complaining about having to vote tomorrow and then my grandmother said something that made me change my opinion about that.

Julie: Really? What did she say?

Cindy: She said:

a ( ) "When I am young, women don't realize they have an option."

b (X) "When I was young, women didn't realize they had an option."

c ( ) "When I had been young, women hadn't realized they had had an option."

d ( ) "When I was young, women realized they had an option."

e ( ) "When I will be young, women will realize they will have an option."

9 "Women can do anything men can do, and do it better... and do it in heels." (*President Barack Obama*)

What is the correct form of indirect speech for this sentence?

a ( ) He said women had done anything men had done, and had done it better and had done it in heels.

b (X) He said women could do anything men could do, and can do it, better and can do it in heels.

c ( ) He said women do anything men do, and do it, better and do it in heels.

d ( ) He said women could do anything men can do, and do it better and do it in heels.

e ( ) He said women did anything men did, and did it, better and did it in heels.

10 The police officer said the girls hadn't shown any signs of being unhappy with the situation.

What is the correct form of direct speech for this sentence?

a ( ) "The girls hadn't shown any signs of being happy with the situation."

b (X) "The girls showed signs of being unhappy with the situation."

c ( ) "The girls don't show any signs of being unhappy with the situation."

d ( ) "The girls didn't show any signs of being unhappy with the situation."

e ( ) "The girls show any signs of being unhappy with the situation."

Refletindo sobre sua aprendizagem

Ao final desta unidade, você já é capaz de:

- Fazer leitura de imagens e relacioná-las ao texto verbal. ☐
- Refletir sobre as diferenças relativas ao progresso rumo à igualdade entre homens e mulheres em diferentes sociedades ao redor do mundo. ☒
- Discutir e expressar pontos de vista sobre conquistas sociais, políticas e econômicas da mulher ao longo dos últimos anos. ☐
- Reconhecer e empregar falsos cognatos. ☒
- Identificar o emprego dos discursos direto e indireto e aplicá-los adequadamente. ☒
- Reconhecer características específicas de publicações digitais. ☐

Aprimorando sua aprendizagem

- Peça ajuda ao professor ou aos colegas para que esclareçam suas dúvidas.
- Refaça os exercícios.
- Visite a biblioteca da sua escola ou uma biblioteca pública e consulte livros de gramática e/ou faça leituras de seu interesse.
- Assista a filmes em inglês.

4 The Way to Success

PRE-READING

Read the title and the section headings. What kind of information do you think you will find in this text?

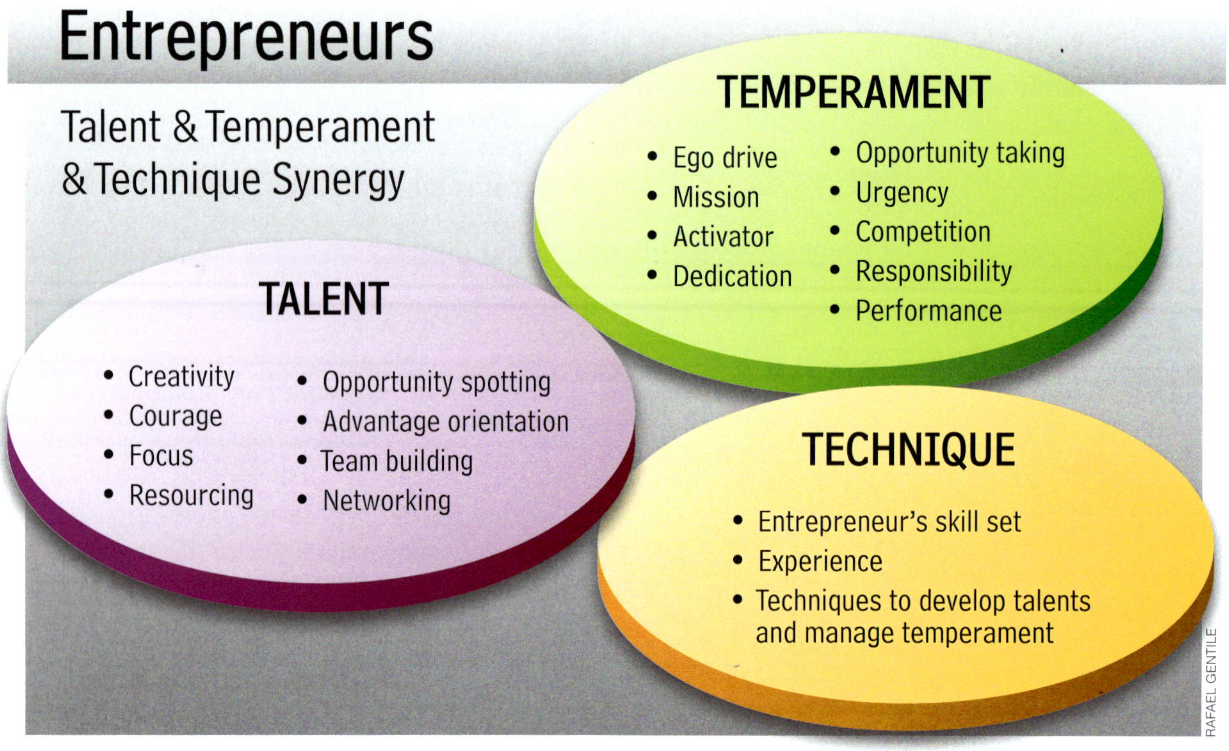

Extracted from <http://www.1000ventures.com/design_elements/selfmade/entrepreneurs_ttt-synergy.gif>. Accessed on February 22, 2010.

"Nobody talks about entrepreneurship as survival, but that's exactly what it is and what nurtures creative thinking. Running that first shop taught me business is not financial science; it's about trading: buying and selling."

Anita Roddick, founder of The Body Shop

"The important thing is not being afraid to take a chance. Remember, the greatest failure is to not try. Once you find something you love to do, be the best at doing it."

Debbie Fields, founder of Mrs. Fields Cookies

Extracted from <http://entrepreneurs.about.com/od/famousentrepreneurs/a/quotations.htm>. Accessed on February 22, 2010.

entrepreneurs: empreendedores
entrepreneurship: empreendedorismo
failure: fracasso
nurtures: estimula
resourcing: provisão de recursos
running: conduzir, dirigir (negócio)
skill set: conjunto de habilidades
spotting: reconhecimento
survival: sobrevivência
take a chance: arriscar
trading: comércio, negócio

After Reading

1 What do we learn from the text? Mark the correct answers.

a ( ) Temperament must be managed through appropriate techniques.
b (✓) Creativity and urgency are talent aspects in entrepreneurship.
c ( ) Business is not something scientific.
d (✓) If you find something you love to do, be outstanding when doing that.
e (✓) Courage and focus are techniques you must develop for entrepreneurship.

2 Who are these ideas related to? Write A for Anita and D for Debbie.

a (A) "Empreendimento é sobrevivência."
b (A) "É importante não ter medo de arriscar."
c (D) "Seja o melhor no que você é bom."
d (A) "O mundo dos negócios não é uma ciência financeira."
e (D) "O grande fracasso é não tentar."
f (A) "O empreendedorismo nutre o pensamento criativo."

3 Find in the text a synonym for each word below.

a bravery	Courage
b imaginativeness	Creatyvity
c background	yard
d need	mission
e commitment	dedication
f endurance	Performance
g commerce	tradding
h breakdown	shutdown
i chance	try
j ability	Skill

RAFAEL GENTILE

4 Leia o extrato de texto abaixo e discuta-o com seus colegas.

Jovens se organizam para estimular empreendedorismo

Ser empreendedor é uma ideia bastante nova, principalmente no Brasil, e ainda pouquíssimo abordada dentro das universidades públicas e privadas, geralmente orientadas para formar futuros profissionais assalariados.

Mas muitos jovens já estão entendendo que desenvolver o próprio espírito empreendedor pode ser uma alternativa mais interessante à busca, cada vez mais difícil, por vagas de emprego com carteira assinada. O assunto ganhou tanta importância que foi formada uma Confederação Nacional dos Jovens Empresários (Conaje) [...].

[...]

A Conaje tem origem nos grupos empresariais de jovens paulistas, gaúchos e mineiros, que se reuniram a partir de 1992 com o intuito de formar lideranças e discutir questões voltadas à construção de uma nova ordem social.

[...]

RAFAEL GENTILE

Extraído de <http://www.hipermeios.com.br/spip.php?article36>.
Acessado em 24 de fevereiro de 2010.

a Você gostaria de ter o seu próprio negócio? Por quê? / Por que não?

b Você conhece pessoas empreendedoras cujos negócios foram bem-sucedidos? Que tipo de negócio essas pessoas tiveram?

c Você sabe quais os principais motivos pelos quais uma empresa abre falência?

Vocabulary in Use

"Once you find something you love to do, be the best **at doing** it."

TIP The **ing form** must be used in verbs that come after a preposition.

1 Fill in the blanks with the correct form of the verb.

a I've advised you **against** ____________ (smoke) in here.

b She's good **at** ____________ (speak) in public.

c I went home **after** ____________ (leave) the party.

d You can improve your English **by** ____________ (use) the internet.

e I'm tired **of** ____________ (hear) excuses.

f Why don't you have something hot to drink **before** ____________ (go) to bed?

g She's always dreamed **about** ____________ (travel) by plane.

h She was promoted **for** ____________ (get) new accounts.

i **Besides** ____________ (be) a doctor, he also writes books.

j I'm looking forward **to** ____________ (meet) you.

2 Complete the sentences below with the prepositions in the box.

about | after | against | at | before | besides | by | for | from | in | of | on | to | up | with

RAFAEL GENTILE

a I'm tired of waiting ______________ him.

b He left the classroom ______________ finishing the exercise.

c Denise prevented me ______________ buying that useless device.

d All of us were familiar ______________ the place, so we didn't get lost.

e We're playing ______________ the champions next Saturday.

f My parents arrived late ______________ the airport, so they couldn't depart.

g Come and sit ______________ me.

h There has been an increase ______________ 20% in this month's sales.

i Leave your books here ______________ you start the test.

j Why don't you come ______________? It's too cold outside.

k Let's talk ______________ that later.

l I walked ______________ the beach, sat, and read for hours.

m ______________ my daughter, I have no family.

n Go ______________ the stairs and take the ball.

o ______________ now on, you should arrive earlier.

Appendix 4 page 155

3 How do you say these sentences in English?

a Eles sempre falam em viajar para a Nova Zelândia.

____

b Susan sonha em ser uma artista de sucesso.

____

Grammar in Use

DIRECT AND INDIRECT SPEECH (II)

<table>
<tr><td>Podemos reportar as perguntas para o discurso indireto de duas formas.</td><td>She said, “Does this restaurant accept credit cards?”
She asked if that restaurant accepted credit cards.

The old man said, “What time is it?”
The old man asked what time it was.</td></tr>
<tr><td colspan="2">Em ambos os casos, as perguntas foram transformadas em frases afirmativas.
As perguntas iniciadas com auxiliares devem apresentar o uso de if (linguagem informal) ou whether (linguagem formal). As perguntas iniciadas com pronomes interrogativos devem repetir seu uso.</td></tr>
<tr><td>Usamos a forma do infinitivo do verbo para relatar ordens ou pedidos expressos pelos verbos ask, tell e order.</td><td>Dad said to us, “Come back home before midnight.”
Dad asked us to come back home before midnight.
Dad told us to come back home before midnight.
Dad ordered us to come back home before midnight.

Dad said to us, “Don’t arrive late again.”
Dad asked us not to arrive late again.</td></tr>
</table>

1 Choose the best alternative to report the questions below.

1.1 “Can you help me with the makeup?”

a ( ) She asked if I could help her with the makeup.

b ( ) She asked if I can help her with the makeup.

1.2 “When does she prefer to start?”

a ( ) The director asked when she prefers to start.

b ( ) The director asked when she preferred to start.

1.3 “Are they changing jobs?”

a ( ) I asked if they were changing jobs.

b ( ) I asked if were they changing jobs.

1.4 “Have you chosen your gift?”

a ( ) They asked me where I had chosen my gift.

b ( ) They asked me if I had chosen my gift.

1.5 “Will you answer my question?”

a ( ) She asked if I would answer my question.

b ( ) She asked if I would answer her question.

2 Match the cartoons to the corresponding indirect speech.

A

B

"Who is John Galt?"

C

D

CARTOONS: WWW.CARTOONSTOCK.COM

E

"This 'Wheel' thing of yours – Does it have to be round or will any shape do?"

F

(B) The man asked who John Galt was.

(A) He asked the actor what he did.

(E) They asked if the wheel had to be round or if any shape would do.

(C) He asked if the man had lived in the district all his life.

(F) The sign on the mirror asked where the man saw himself the next day.

(d) The boy asked the coach if he could be in the goal.

3 Rewrite the orders below as indirect speech.

a The wife said to her husband, “Don’t cheat on me!”

The wife ordered her husband to don't cheat on her! ______.

b The police officers said to the men, “Let the women leave the dangerous area first.”

The police officers asked the men to let the women leave the... ______.

c The mother said to her daughter, “Brush your teeth.”

The mother told her daughter to brushe her teeth ______.

d The girl said to her puppy, “Jump!”

The girl ordered her puppy ______.

e My boss said to me, “Don’t use the company phone for private calls.”

My boss told me ______.

f The chef said to the cook, “Sprinkle less oregano on the pizza.”

The chef asked the cook ______.

4 Change these sentences from indirect to direct speech.

a Dan asked Sylvia what her favorite color was.

Dan asked Sylvia, what is your favorite color?

b Mom told us to obey the classroom rules.

Mom said to us, obey the classroom rules

c Grace asked what time the game show would start.

Grace asked, When the game is starting

d Alan told his little brother not to believe strangers.

Alan said to his little brother, Don't believe in strangers

e The cop ordered the citizens to stay away from the crime scene.

The cop said to the citizens, stay away from the crime scene f Grandma asked me if I enjoyed playing video games.

Grandma asked me,

g I asked them if they had watched the game on TV the day before.

I asked them,

5 Below you will find extracts from Anita's and Debbie's quotes on page 52. Transform them into indirect speech.

a "Nobody talks about entrepreneurship as survival."

Anita said ____________________.

b "Running that first shop taught me business is not financial science."

Anita said ____________________.

c "The important thing is not being afraid to take a chance."

Debbie said that ____________________.

d "The greatest failure is to not try."

Debbie said ____________________.

6 Write full answers to the questions below. Use indirect speech.

a What did your dad say to you when you failed the finals?

____

____

b What did your Geography teacher tell you to do for the monthly project?

____

____

c What did your best friend ask you to do for his or her birthday party?

____

____

Reading

File Edit View Favorites Tools Help

Address http://www.alliancemagazine.org/node/3149 Go Links »

Search

Latin America News

Brazilian entrepreneur among the best philanthropists, according to *Barron's* and the Global Philanthropy Group

December 15, 2009
www.alliancemagazine.org

When the situation gets tough, philanthropists must try to do more with less. As a result, the use of donations becomes more relevant. A list published in early December reveals "the best of the best", in a selection made by the *Barron's* business publication in collaboration with the Global Philanthropy Group consulting firm. The 25 best donors of the year, in terms of the quality of results obtained (rather than the quantity), were chosen according to criteria such as innovation, the quality of alliances with other groups, the effects of donations, and the possibility of replicating successful projects.

This list includes Brazilian entrepreneur Marcos de Moraes, president of the Sagatiba drinks company. De Moraes sold his ZipNet Company (which represented the largest computer business transaction ever in Brazil) a few years ago, and started the Rukha Institute, an NGO to help at-risk children and their families. "Many people tell me that it is risky to invest so much in an NGO. But it is worse to have the opportunity to help and not do anything," says De Moraes.

Start

Extracted from <http://www.alliancemagazine.org/node/3149>.
Accessed on February 22, 2010.

alliances: alianças, coligações
at-risk: em risco
criteria: critérios
donors: doadores
philanthropists: filantropos
rather than: em vez de
reveals: revela
risky: arriscado
tough: difícil, complexa

After Reading

1 Read the text on page 60 again and choose the best alternative.

1.1 When a situation is unfavorable, philanthropists:

a ( ) ignore obstacles and don't try anything new.
b (X) make the best of what they have.
c ( ) don't keep their projects and start a new business.

1.2 Which item is ***not*** part of the criteria for the selection of the 25 best donors of the year?

a ( ) New methods and ideas.
b (X) Making repeated use of effective projects.
c ( ) Investments in annual shows and fairs.

1.3 The Brazilian entrepreneur Marcos de Moraes:

a ( ) opened a new computer company in South America.
b (X) is responsible for a non-profit organization.
c ( ) doesn't think NGOs are important anymore.

2 Read the following sentence taken from the text.

"When the situation **gets** tough, philanthropists must try to do more with less."

Get is one of the most common words in English. If you take a look at this word in a dictionary, you'll see there are different meanings. In the sentence above, **gets** means **becomes**.

Now choose a synonym for the word **get** in the sentences below. Use the words in the box.

receives	arrive	buy	become	understand	picks up

a Sometimes my sister gets our dinner on her way home from work. Picks up

b I need to get a new webcam because mine is out of order. buy

c It takes me more than an hour to get to school in the morning. arrive

d I'm sure Professor Smart will get angry if Jenny doesn't take the test today. become

e Can you repeat what you said about the school team? I didn't get it. understand

f Ms. Taylor gets lots of e-mails from clients all over the world. receives

3 Volte ao texto da página 60, responda às perguntas abaixo e reconheça algumas das características do gênero textual notícia.

a Qual é o objetivo da notícia apresentada?

Informar sobre a filantropia e contar a história de Marcos

b A quem a notícia é destinada?

Ao público em geral

c Você pode observar na notícia alguma passagem que demonstre a opinião pessoal de quem a escreveu? Se sua resposta for positiva, transcreva a passagem que a fundamente.

"In terms of quality of results obtained (rather than quantity)"

d Onde ela foi veiculada? Em que data?

Aliance magazine, 15/12/2009

e Em qual parágrafo podemos encontrar informações fundamentais da notícia?

2

f É comum os jornalistas citarem o discurso de algumas pessoas. Isso acontece nessa notícia? Em qual parágrafo?

3

g Como o leitor pode identificar esse discurso de terceiros?

Aspas

RAFAEL GENTILE

Consultando outras fontes

filmes: *À procura da felicidade* (EUA, 2006; direção: Gabriele Muccino)
Jerry Maguire – A grande virada (EUA, 1996; direção: Cameron Crowe)

livros: *Você está louco!* (Rocco; autor: Ricardo Semler)
Virando a própria mesa (Rocco; autor: Ricardo Semler)

Baking and Pastry Arts Professionals

PHOTO: STOCKFOLIO® / ALAMY / OTHER IMAGES; ART: RAFAEL GENTILE

When thinking about entrepreneurship, we immediately picture a very big conglomerate with thousands of employees and profits of millions each year, right? Well, you don't need to go that far to be an entrepreneur. Besides, a good number of organizations started out as small businesses and got growing step by step.

There are many easier ways for you to get started. How about your own kitchen with little or no money at all? Yes, you can become a baking and pastry chef right now.

Baking and pastry chefs prepare, flavor, and cook many different kinds of cakes, biscuits, petit fours, pastries, sugar, and marzipan sweets, chocolate goods, and both cold and warm desserts, as well as traditional and artistic breads, croissants, tarts, pies, doughnuts, Danish pastries, and whatever else their creativity and imagination may lead them to.

These professionals need to be aware of and maintain a healthy and safe food preparation environment by following legal standards and procedures and complying with legal and sanitary regulations.

ICEAL / SHUTTERSTOCK

Needless to say, you don't really need a diploma to get started with your baking and pastry business, but it helps a lot to develop some cooking skills and learn about food conservation, flavor combinations, icing, sauce and cream preparation, as well as all the regulations involved in cooking.

If you want a head-start in this business, you can take a baking and pastry technical course. It's only 800 to 1200 hours long (depending on the vocational school you choose) and you can take it while you're still in high school.

Good luck on all your endeavors!

Based on <http://www.continente.ifsc.edu.br/novo/index.php?option=com_content&view=article&id=92&Itemid=29>; <http://cursostecnicos.sedu.es.gov.br/?target=curso_visualiza&cid=88>; <http://www.careeroverview.com/chef-careers.html>; <http://www.jobprofiles.org/retpastrychef.htm>. Accessed on February 27, 2010.

be aware of: estar ciente de, ter consciência de
complying with: estar em conformidade com
conglomerate: conglomerado (de empresas)
Danish pastries: bolos doces feitos de massa leve, geralmente contendo maçã, nozes, etc., e cobertos com glacê
endeavors: empenho; tentativa
flavor: sabor
needless to say: desnecessário dizer
pastry chef: confeiteiro

Você gostaria de ser técnico em panificação e confeitaria? Por quê? / Por que não?

Não. Por que toma muito tempo / determinação.

Additional Practice

For exercises 1 to 8, choose the best alternative.

1 The viability of ________ in today's market scenario is debatable, but it never stopped anybody from trying.

a (   ) philanthropist
b (   ) nurture
c (   ) trading
d (   ) failure
e (   ) entrepreneurship

2 My company opened an office in Hamburg, one of Europe's largest import-and-export cities, which has a long tradition in ________ goods worldwide.

a (   ) philanthropist
b (   ) nurture
c (   ) trading
d (   ) failure
e (   ) entrepreneurship

3 "When it comes to good causes, Eva Longoria is all business. The *Desperate Housewives* star was just named ________ of the Year by *The Hollywood Reporter* and she's spreading goodwill in Miami Beach Saturday for the Rally for Children with Cancer. [...]"

Extracted from <http://www.miamiherald.com/2009/11/20/1343125/eva-longoria-parker-is-a-helpful.html>. Accessed on January 24, 2010.

a (   ) Philanthropist
b (   ) Nurture
c (   ) Trading
d (   ) Failure
e (   ) Entrepreneurship

4 "Don Keough, the former Coca-Cola president who sits on Warren Buffett's Berkshire Hathaway board, is often invited to speak about business success. But he elected to call his book *The Ten Commandments for Business* ________ [...]"

Extracted from <http://www.usatoday.com/money/companies/management/advice/2009-01-18-don-keough-advice-coke_N.htm>. Accessed on January 23, 2010.

a (   ) *Philanthropists*
b (   ) *Nurture*
c (   ) *Trading*
d (   ) *Failure*
e (   ) *Entrepreneurship*

5 The government intends to develop a collaborative network of schools that ________ success among underprivileged children.

a (   ) philanthropists
b (   ) nurture
c (   ) trading
d (   ) failure
e (   ) entrepreneurship

6 I remember listening to my father telling me about how he started his own company. He ________ me to take risks and do things that no one has ever done before.

a (   ) said
b (   ) told
c (   ) order
d (   ) tell
e (   ) says

7 **You:** I talked to the founder of this new company that manufactures nano materials and I think I'm going to invest in them.

Your spouse: Don't invest all your money in a single company!

a (   ) My spouse told me to don't invest all my money in a single company.
b (   ) My spouse told me don't invest all your money in a single company.
c (   ) My spouse asks me not to invest all my money in a single company.
d (   ) My spouse ordered me not to invest all my money in a single company.
e (   ) My spouse said to invest all my money in a single company.

8 **You:** I've been thinking about opening my own business. But I don't have the necessary funds to start.

Mr. Hendricks: How much money do you need to start your business?

a ( ) Mr. Hendricks told me how much money do I need to start my business.
b (X) Mr. Hendricks asked me how much money I needed to start my business.
c ( ) Mr. Hendricks ordered me how much money I needed to start my business.
d ( ) Mr. Hendricks said how much money I needed to start my business.
e ( ) Mr. Hendricks told me how much money I needed to start my business.

9 Sometime ago, my cousin Bob asked me what was wrong with the Americans.
What did my cousin Bob say?

a ( ) "What was wrong with the Americans?"
b (X) "What is wrong with the Americans?"
c ( ) "What has been wrong with the Americans?"
d ( ) "What had been wrong with the Americans?"
e ( ) "What could be wrong with the Americans?"

10 The negative form for the sentence "My boss told me to leave the company to start my own business" is:

a ( ) "My boss told me not to leave the company to start my own business."
b ( ) "My boss told me don't leave the company to start your own business."
c (X) "My boss told me to not leave the company to start my own business."
d ( ) "My boss told me to didn't leave the company to start my own business."
e ( ) "My boss didn't tell me not to leave the company to start my own business."

Refletindo sobre sua aprendizagem

Ao final desta unidade, você já é capaz de:

- Reconhecer características necessárias a um empreendedor bem-sucedido. ☐
- Identificar sinônimos para palavras relacionadas ao tema empreendedorismo. ☐
- Refletir sobre as vantagens e desvantagens de ter um negócio próprio. ☐
- Assimilar e aplicar o uso do gerúndio dos verbos (*ing form*) após preposições. ☐
- Identificar o emprego dos discursos direto e indireto quando relativos a perguntas, pedidos e ordens e aplicá-los adequadamente. ☐
- Observar os diferentes significados da palavra *get* e utilizá-los de maneira adequada ao contexto em que estão inseridos. ☐
- Identificar características do gênero textual notícia. ☐

Aprimorando sua aprendizagem

- Peça ajuda ao professor ou aos colegas para que esclareçam suas dúvidas.
- Refaça os exercícios.
- Visite a biblioteca da sua escola ou uma biblioteca pública e consulte livros de gramática e/ou faça leituras de seu interesse.
- Assista a filmes em inglês.

Language in Action 2

1 Discuss the following statements with a classmate.

- Women should stay home with the children.
- Women are better than men at looking after children.
- Women are more dedicated to jobs than men.
- Women can have children and a career.
- Women need to earn a lot of money at work to be successful.
- Women prefer working outside the home.
- Women and men should be paid the same amount of money for the same jobs.

RAFAEL GENTILE

2 Read the newspaper advice column below. What's Nick's problem? What kind of advice would you give him?

Advice column

My name's Nick. My wife runs her own business. To me, she's a workaholic. She goes to her office very early in the morning and doesn't come back home before nine or ten p.m. She works seven days a week and usually brings work home. We rarely go out with friends, but when we do, she spends the night talking about her job. We haven't traveled on holidays for the past three years and when I sit down to talk to her about this, she says she can't make any plans. What should I do?

RAFAEL GENTILE

3 Listen to three women talking about their problems. Identify each one's problem.

BILL VARIE / CORBIS-LATINSTOCK

Helen

WORMDOG51 / SHUTTERSTOCK

Sara

GUY MODERLY / ALAMY-OTHER IMAGES

Amanda

Writing

What kind of advice would you give the women? Write a short note to each.

RAFAEL GENTILE

Dear Helen,

Dear Amanda,

Dear Sara,

5 The Pleasure of Reading

PRE-READING

Do you know the books below? Who wrote them?

Jorge Amado

[...]

Amado's literary works have been adapted to the screen, stage, and television countless times, and are even the theme of Carnival parades throughout Brazil. His books have been translated into 49 languages and published in 55 countries. There are also copies available in Braille and on tape for the blind.

The Jorge Amado House Foundation officially opened in Salvador's Largo do Pelourinho in 1987. Since then, it has housed his library and made it available to researchers. The foundation also aims to develop cultural activities in Bahia. [. . .]

Extracted from <http://www.jorgeamado.org.br/ing/jorge_biografia.htm>. Accessed on February 10, 2010.

Captains of the Sands

It tells the story of Bahia street children in the 30s. A love story about Dora and Pedro Bala. The exploits of a band of youths who rove the dangerous streets and docklands of Salvador, a "black and religious" city, in which *ialorixá* Aninha, high priestess of the Candomblé temple Ilê Axé Opô Afonjá, is a powerful presence. Dora falls ill and dies in the moonlit warehouse. Pedro Bala is arrested, escapes, and gets involved in dock workers' strikes, eventually becoming a "proletarian militant, comrade Pedro Bala."

[. . .]

Extracted from <http://www.fundacaojorgeamado.com.br/ing/obras_jorge/capitaes2.htm>. Accessed on February 10, 2010.

Gabriela, Clove, and Cinnamon

The beloved Brazilian classic from the acclaimed author of *Dona Flor and Her Two Husbands*. One spring day in 1925, a disheveled Gabriela arrives in the seaside port of Ilhéus and takes a job as cook in a local establishment in desperate need. Soon, the proprietor finds that he has the best business in town and that he employs the most sought-after woman.

Extracted from <http://www.goodreads.com/book/show/91659.Gabriela_Clove_and_Cinnamon>. Accessed on February 10, 2010.

beloved: amado
countless: inúmeras
disheveled: desalinhada, de cabelos soltos
docklands: cais do porto
exploits: façanhas, proezas
rove: perambulavam
sought-after: muito procurada, em grande demanda
warehouse: armazém

After Reading

1 Take a look at the text. Find eight transparent words and one false cognate.

Transparent words	False cognate

RAFAEL GENTILE

2 Read the text again and find the words that correspond to the definitions below.

a a temporary stoppage of activities in protest against an act or condition ____________

b a woman authorized to perform the sacred rites of a religion ____________

c a continual passing by, as of people, objects, or events ____________

d the plan or main story, as of a movie or literary work ____________

e unable to see ____________

f a fictitious narrative portraying characters and presenting a sequential organization of action and scenes ____________

3 According to the text, we can infer that:

a ( ) the social situation of Bahia has always been of richness and abundance.

b ( ) *Captains of the Sands* also tells the story of Gabriela.

c ( ) Jorge Amado's literary works are of the greatest importance to literature in worldwide.

d ( ) Carnival parades have never celebrated Jorge Amado's work.

4 Leia o extrato de texto abaixo e discuta-o com seus colegas.

[...]

Gerações de décadas passadas eram sedentas por leitura, contudo, apesar do interesse, muitas delas não possuíam condições financeiras de adquirirem conhecimento através dos livros. Antigamente, tinha-se mais filhos, poucos estudavam devido ao fato de que todos deveriam trabalhar para assegurar o sustento da família. O que ocorre com a geração atual é justamente o contrário: os jovens de hoje concentram grande poder financeiro em suas carteiras, porém, usufruem deste privilégio consumindo somente aquilo que está na moda. Adquirem roupas de marcas e celulares com funções "multissupérfluas" em vez de investirem em sua cultura de "multiconhecimento". Ignoram as boas obras literárias, considerando-as "ultrapassadas". Frequentam academias em busca do corpo que não lhes pertence, ao invés de visitarem uma biblioteca e exercitar seus neurônios. Nada mais justo do que fazer seu cérebro "puxar ferro" também.

[...]

RAFAEL GENTILE

Extraído de <http://www.midiaindependente.org/pt/blue/2005/09/328545.shtml>. Acessado em 24 de fevereiro de 2010.

a Você acha importante ler? Por quê? / Por que não?

b Você acha importante os jovens conhecerem a cultura de seu país?

c Você concorda com o artigo a respeito de como os jovens atuais gastam seu dinheiro?

d Na sua opinião, quais são os motivos que contribuem para o declínio do hábito da leitura entre os jovens brasileiros?

Vocabulary in Use

1 Read the dictionary entry and do the activity.

literature writings in which expression and form, in connection with ideas of permanent and universal interest, are characteristic or essential features, as poetry, novels, history, biography, and essays.

ANDREZA MOREIRA

Extracted from <http://dictionary.reference.com/browse/literature>. Accessed on March 1, 2010.

Here are some genres of literary works. Choose the best word from the box for the definitions below. You can use the glossary if necessary. Some words will not be used.

autobiography | drama | epistle | essay
fable | fairy tale | horror
limerick | memoir | romance | saga
satire | sonnet | tragedy

RAFAEL GENTILE

a a kind of humorous verse of five lines, in which the first, second, and fifth lines rhyme with each other, and the third and fourth lines, which are shorter, form a rhymed couplet ____________

b a letter, especially a formal or didactic one; written communication ____________

c a record of events written by a person having intimate knowledge of them and based on personal observation ____________

d any narrative or legend of heroic exploits ____________

e a short tale to teach a moral lesson, often with animals or inanimate objects as characters ____________

f a story, usually for children, about elves, hobgoblins, dragons, fairies, or other magical creatures ____________

g any situation or series of events having vivid, emotional, conflicting, or striking interest or results ____________

h a history of a person's life written or told by that person ____________

i a dramatic composition, often in verse, dealing with a serious or somber theme, typically that of a great person destined through a flaw of character or conflict with some overpowering force, as fate or society, to downfall or destruction ____________

j a literary composition, in verse or prose, in which human folly and vice are held up to scorn, derision, or ridicule ____________

Extracted from <http://dictionary.reference.com>. Accessed on February 10, 2010.

Grammar in Use

FUTURE PERFECT

FORMAÇÃO: **WILL HAVE** + PARTICÍPIO DO VERBO PRINCIPAL

Forma afirmativa	The Jorge Amado Foundation **will have developed** several cultural activities by 2020.
Forma negativa	The story of Gabriela and Nacib Saad in *Gabriela, Clove, and Cinnamon* **won't (will + not) have ceased** to enchant readers by the next decades.
Forma interrogativa	**Will** many people **have read** *Captains of the Sands* by 10 years from now? Yes, they will. / No, they won't.

USO

O **Future Perfect** é utilizado para expressar uma ação que terá (ou não) acontecido antes de um determinado momento no futuro.	The students **will have finished** the project by the end of the month.

Nota

O **Future Continuous** (will be + verbo + ing) expressa uma ação que estará ocorrendo em um determinado tempo no futuro.	I **will be working** next weekend.

1 Complete the sentences below with the verbs in parentheses. Use the Future Perfect.

a How much ________ you ________ (spend) by the end of the month?

b By the time I go to bed tonight, I ________ (work) for 12 hours.

c Unfortunately, by the end of the spring, Jane ________ (lose – neg.) all the weight she put on last summer.

d How many glasses of water ________ she ________ (drink) by the end of a day?

e They ________ (buy) several unnecessary items by the time I meet them at the supermarket.

f By the time you're 70, you ________ (read) hundreds of books.

g If they continue spending that much, they ________ (spend) all their holiday money by the end of the week.

h The builder says that he ________ (finish) the roof of my house by Friday.

2 What will the children have done by the end of the school day? Look at the picture and complete the sentences. Use the expressions in the box.

VICENTE MENDONÇA

buy candies	draw and color	drink her juice	eat his snack
play tag	go down the slide	jump rope	talk to the teacher

a Three girls ______________________________ beautiful pictures.

b Two boys and one girl ______________________________.

c A little boy ______________________________.

d Two girls ______________________________.

e A boy and a girl ______________________________.

f A girl ______________________________.

g Another boy ______________________________.

h A girl ______________________________.

3 Rewrite the sentences. Use the cues in parentheses.

a She will have flown to the U.S. by April.

(int.) Will she have flown to the U.S by April?

b The passengers will have forgotten all about the accident by the time they reach their final destination.

(neg.) the passengers won't have forgotten all About the accident?

c We will have eaten our lunch by two o'clock.

(int.) Will we have eaten our lunch by two o'clock

d Will he have sold his old motorcycle by the end of the week?

(aff.) he will have sold his old motorcycle by the end of the week

e You will have saved enough to go to Spain by December.

(neg.) Will you have saved enough to go to Spain by december?

f Will they have rested by the end of the day?

(aff.) they will have rested by the end of the day?

4 Use the expression *by the time* to join the sentences below. The first one is done for you.

a I will do my Chemistry project next weekend. The teacher will ask for that project next month.

By the time the teacher asks for my Chemistry project, I will have done it.

b Dennis will leave São Paulo at 5:00 p.m. Joana will arrive at 6:00 p.m.

By the time dennis will leave São paulo At 5:00 p.m. Joana will arrive At 6:00 p.m

c Surya will have breakfast at the bakery. Emir will go shopping at lunch-time.

By the time Surya will have breakfast At the bakery. Emir will go shopping At lunch-time

d The doctor will arrive at the clinic at noon. The secretary will leave the clinic at 2 p.m.

By the time the doctor arrive At the clinic At noon. the secretary will leave the clinic At 2. p.m

e I will go to the movies at 4:00 p.m. My parents will talk to the principal at the end of the day.

By the time my parets will talk to the principal At the end of the day. I will go to the movies At 4:00 pm

5 What do you think will have happened in the next fifty years? Write sentences with the cues given. You can write affirmative or negative sentences.

a The pandas / become / extinct

the pandas won't have become extinct

b Brazil / find / oil / in the Amazon

Brazil will have find oil in the Amazon

c Scientists / discover / the cure for obesity

Scientists will have discover the cure for obesity

d Men / travel / to Mars

Men will have travel to Mars

e Nuclear weapons / be extinguished

Nuclear weapons will have be extinguished

f Books / disappear

Books won't have disappear.

6 Choose the best verb form to complete the sentences.

6.1 Do your best on your exam. Here, I ________ for your success.

a (X) will be praying **b** ( ) will have prayed

6.2 By this time tomorrow, we ________ lunch with our family members.

a ( ) will have **b** (X) will have had

6.3 She hopes I ________ the cookies by the time she arrives so I can help her with the cake.

a ( ) will be baking **b** (X) will have baked

6.4 Don't even try to get in touch with me on my vacation. I ________ in Europe.

a (X) will be traveling **b** ( ) will have traveled

6.5 Teacher, we promise we ________ all your expectations by the end of the semester.

a ( ) will be meeting **b** (X) will have met

6.6 Hurry up! If not, the plane ________ by the time you get to the airport.

a ( ) will be leaving **b** (X) will have left

6.7 By this time next Monday, Dan ________ happily with his new co-workers.

a (X) will be talking **b** ( ) will talk

Reading

Vinicius de Moraes, *o poetinha* (the little poet) (October 19, 1913 – July 9, 1980), born Marcus Vinicius da Cruz de Melo Moraes in Rio de Janeiro, Brazil, was a seminal figure in contemporary Brazilian music. As a poet, he wrote lyrics for a great number of songs that became all-time classics. He was also a composer, a playwright, a diplomat, and as an interpreter of his own songs, he left several important albums.

[...]

Extracted from <http://youmix.co.uk/bio/11215>. Accessed on February 15, 2010.

Sonnet of Fidelity

Vinicius de Moraes

Above all, to my love I'll be attentive
First and always, with care and so much
That even when facing the greatest enchantment
By love be more enchanted my thoughts.

I want to live it through in each vain moment
And in its honor I'll spread my song
And laugh my laughter and cry my tears
When you are sad or when you are content.

And thus, when later comes looking for me
Who knows, the death, anxiety of the living
Who knows, the loneliness, end of all lovers.

I'll be able to say to myself of the love (I had):
Be not immortal, since it is flame
But be infinite while it lasts.

Extracted from <http://oldpoetry.com/opoem/119640-Vinicius-de-Moraes-Sonnet-of-Fidelity>. Accessed on February 15, 2010.

enchantment: encantamento

flame: chama

loneliness: solidão

playwright: dramaturgo, autor de peças teatrais

seminal: original

tears: pranto

thus: deste modo

vain: vão, fútil

After Reading

1 Read these quotes from people talking about relationships. Which of them matches the last stanza of the poem?

RAFAEL GENTILE

a (X) I did like him a lot. For a long time I thought of him all the time and thought I would marry him one day. But then it ended.
Louise (21)

b ( ) I don't want to get involved. If I feel the other person is getting too attached I stop seeing him or her.
Marcus (28)

c ( ) Love never dies. It changes, takes on another pace and format, but lasts forever.
Hugh (35)

Appendix 5 page 156

2 Na página 68 você leu dois resumos de obras famosas de Jorge Amado. O gênero textual resumo traz a apresentação concisa de aspectos relevantes de um texto, é composto predominantemente de frases afirmativas e, geralmente, é organizado em parágrafo único.

Leia o resumo do livro *A arca de Noé*, de Vinicius de Moraes, e faça os exercícios abaixo.

RAFAEL GENTILE

A arca de Noé é também o título do primeiro poema desse livro. O conjunto é formado por 32 poemas, a maioria sobre bichos, e inclui os que constam dos discos *Arca de Noé 1* e *2*. Alguns foram musicados pelo próprio Vinicius de Moraes (1913-80) e se tornaram clássicos da MPB para crianças. (Um bom exemplo é o daquela casa "muito engraçada" que "não tinha teto não tinha nada".) Todos são poemas feitos para ler, aprender de cor ou cantar. Prêmio Jabuti 1992 de Melhor Produção Editorial de Obra em Coleção.

Extraído de <http://www.travessa.com.br/A_ARCA_DE_NOE/artigo/e96ac98e-f779-4d0a-aade-34794d7fe880>.
Acessado em 15 de fevereiro de 2010.

2.1 Aponte as informações mais importantes nas seguintes obras:

a *Capitães da Areia*

Menino de rua na Bahia

b *Gabriela, Cravo e Canela*

Romance entre Nacibe e gabriela

c *A arca de Noé*

Sobre bichos

2.2 Cite as semelhanças entre os três resumos no que diz respeito à sua apresentação.

Que tem uma conotação artistica

Consultando outras fontes

CDs: *A arte de Vinicius de Moraes* (Vinicius de Moraes)
Jorge Amado – Letra e música (Jorge Amado)

filme: *Vinicius* (Brasil, 2005; direção: Miguel Faria Jr. e Suzana Moraes)

livros: *Capitães da areia* (Record; autor: Jorge Amado)
Terras do sem-fim (Record; autor: Jorge Amado)
Antologia poética de Vinicius de Moraes (Companhia das Letras; organização: A. Cícero e E. Ferraz)

Editor

PELLETIER MICHELINE / CORBIS SYGMA / LATINSTOCK; ART: RAFAEL GENTILE

When you read a book, a magazine, or anything written, most of the time you don't realize that you're not only reading the words.

Editors work together with the authors of the text and take care of all the visual aspects – coloring, font, pictures, font size – you name it. And that's not all. These professionals are also in charge of supervising the production process, as well as taking care of deadlines and budgets. They even get a say about the quality of the information that's being published.

If you become an editor, you may work with publishing houses, communication, publicity, and web-design companies, or with any institution where books, journals, magazines, textbooks, manuals, pamphlets, brochures, posters, and flyers are created. You may also work with image treatment.

In order to become an editor, a person has to take a four-year course. Eight semesters is definitely not much, if you consider the fact that the market is expanding and there are more opportunities for editors every day.

Based on <http://guiadoestudante.abril.com.br/profissoes/comunicacao-informacao/profissoes_279861.shtml>; <http://online.onetcenter.org/link/summary/27-3041.00>; <www.wisegeek.com/what-does-an-editor-in-chief-do.htm>; <www.buzzle.com/articles/editor-in-chief-responsibilities.html>; <http://diplomaguide.com/articles/Editor_In_Chief_Career_Overview.html>. Accessed on February 5, 2010.

brochures: folhetos, brochuras
budgets: orçamentos
deadlines: prazos
flyers: filipetas
get a say: opinam
realize: percebe

Você gostaria de trabalhar em produção editorial? Por quê? / Por que não?

Additional Practice

For exercises 1 to 10, choose the best alternative.

1 **Son:** Dad, do we have the book *Captains of the Sands* at home? I have to read it for school.

Dad: I read *Captains of the Sands* _______ times when I was a teenager. Jorge Amado is one of my favorite writers.

a ( ) screen
b ( ) stage
c ( ) throughout
d ( ) blind
e (X) countless

2 _______ his career, Jorge Amado was awarded many important prizes, such as the Camões Prize, the most important literary award of the Portuguese language.

a (X) Screen
b ( ) Stage
c ( ) Throughout
d ( ) Blind
e ( ) Outsiders

3 "*Gabriela, Clove, and Cinnamon* is a delicious and delightful novel that takes place in the Brazilian town of Ilhéus in the mid 1920s. The _______ centers on the romance between the bar owner Nacib, the Arab, and the graceful Gabriela, a mulatto beauty that is willing to work as Nacib's cook for next to nothing because she is running away from famine [...]."

Extracted from <http://search.barnesandnoble.com/Gabriela-Clove-and-Cinnamon/Jorge-Amado/e/9780307276650>. Accessed on January 24, 2010.

a ( ) houses
b (X) aims
c ( ) plot
d ( ) priest
e ( ) captivating

4 The actress Sonia Braga was much _______ after when *Gabriela, Clove, and Cinnamon* was adapted to television.

a ( ) talkative
b (X) sought
c ( ) homeless
d ( ) shy
e ( ) unhappy

5 Gabriela is a migrant worker from an _______ town in the countryside and Nacib Saad owns a bar.

a (X) housed
b ( ) impoverished
c ( ) homeless
d ( ) stage
e ( ) outsiders

6 Jorge Amado's old residence now _______ the Jorge Amado House Foundation, where there are many writing workshops. Jorge didn't want this place to be a depository for old books and documents.

a ( ) houses
b ( ) aims
c ( ) screen
d ( ) priest
e (X) captivating

7 "[...]

The Spanish Repertory Theater took the 1966 Jorge Amado novel *Dona Flor e Seus Dois Maridos* (*Dona Flor and Her Two Husbands*), adapted it to Spanish from the original Portuguese, added a Latin American TV and film star, and found a hit.

[...]

The 1976 movie version helped make an international star of Sonia Braga as Flor and became the most successful film in Brazilian history. For the stage adaptation, the ________ ignored the film, dropping some of its gags, and went back to Amado's text. [...]"

Extracted from <http://www.reuters.com/article/idUSN1533031620080517>. Accessed on January 24, 2010.

a ( ) countless
b ( ) priest
c ( ) seminal
d (X) wealthy
e ( ) playwrights

8 We hope that by the end of 2050, more than a thousand plays ________ in this new theater.

a ( ) will be staged
b (X) will have being staged
c ( ) have been staged
d ( ) will be being staged
e ( ) will have been staged

9 **Betty:** The priest of our church is going to retire. He told me the news himself.
Mrs. Law: Oh, how sad! Well, he's been working there for 43 years. I think it's time for him to retire.
Betty: He doesn't know who is going to take his place, but he ________ by the end of this year.

a ( ) will replace
b ( ) will have being replaced
c ( ) will have been replaced
d ( ) will be being replaced
e (X) will have been replace

10 **Mick:** I read in the news today about a potential cure for blindness, using a retina implant prototype modeled after digital camera technology.

Cesar: That's great news!

Mick: Yeah. If this implant is successful, thousands of blind people ________ by the end of the century.

a (X) will cure
b ( ) will have being cured
c ( ) will have be cured
d ( ) will have been cured
e ( ) have been cured

Refletindo sobre sua aprendizagem

Ao final desta unidade, você já é capaz de:

- Identificar as principais características do gênero textual resumo. ☐
- Reconhecer palavras transparentes e falsos cognatos em textos. ☐
- Discutir a importância da leitura para a formação de capital cultural. ☐
- Identificar diferentes gêneros literários. ☐
- Assimilar forma e uso do *Future Perfect* e empregá-lo em contextos adequados. ☐

Aprimorando sua aprendizagem

- Peça ajuda ao professor ou aos colegas para que esclareçam suas dúvidas.
- Refaça os exercícios.
- Visite a biblioteca da sua escola ou uma biblioteca pública e consulte livros de gramática e/ou faça leituras de seu interesse.
- Assista a filmes em inglês.

6 Fighting the Flu

PRE-READING

What kind of text is this? Where was it published?

File Edit View Favorites Tools Help

Address http://www.cdc.gov/h1n1flu/qa.htm Go Links »

Search

QUESTIONS AND ANSWERS

2009 H1N1 Flu ("Swine Flu") and You

February 10, 2010

What is 2009 H1N1 ("swine flu")?

2009 H1N1 (sometimes called "swine flu") is a new influenza virus causing illness in people. This new virus was first detected in people in the United States in April 2009. This virus is spreading from person-to-person worldwide, probably in much the same way that regular seasonal influenza viruses spread. On June 11, 2009, the World Health Organization (WHO) signaled that a pandemic of 2009 H1N1 flu was underway.

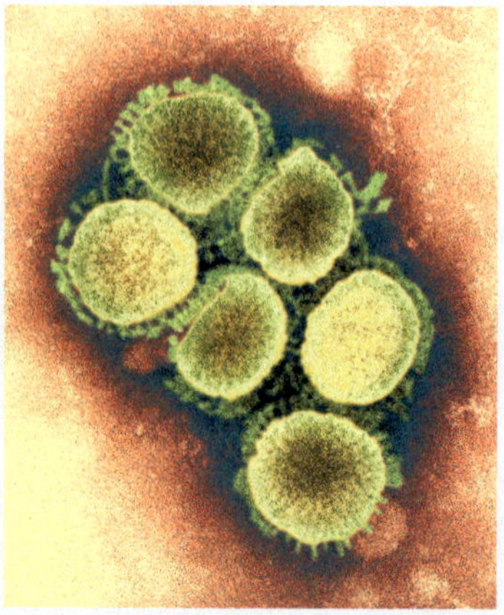

Why is 2009 H1N1 virus sometimes called "swine flu"?

This virus was originally referred to as "swine flu" because laboratory testing showed that many of the genes in this new virus were very similar to influenza viruses that normally occur in pigs (swine) in North America. But further study has shown that this new virus is very different from what normally circulates in North American pigs. It has two genes from flu viruses that normally circulate in pigs in Europe and Asia and bird (avian) genes and human genes. Scientists call this a "quadruple reassortant" virus.

Start

Extracted from <http://www.cdc.gov/h1n1flu/qa.htm>. Accessed on January 28, 2010.

avian: aviária, relativa às aves

influenza: gripe

quadruple reassortant virus: vírus recombinante quádruplo

spreading: espalhando

underway: encaminhado, em andamento

After Reading

1 According to the picture below, what is the most unusual way of infection? Check the correct answer.

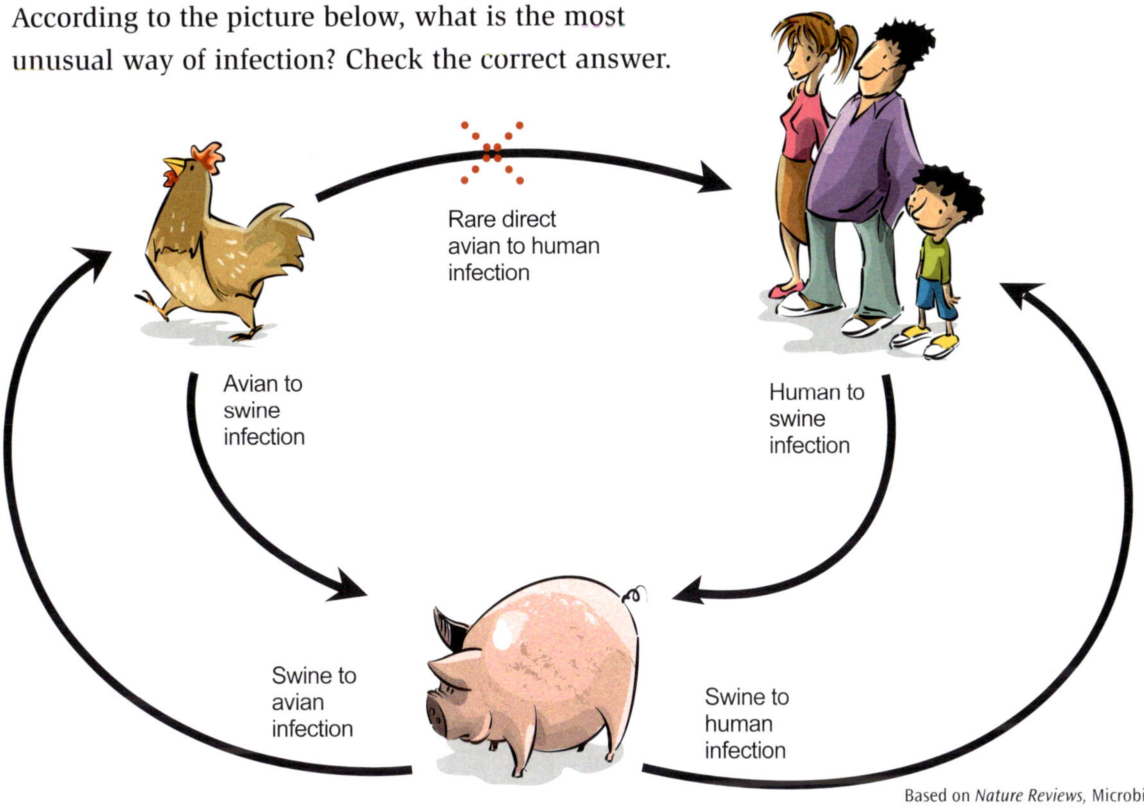

ILLUSTRATIONS: VICENTE MENDONÇA

Based on *Nature Reviews*, Microbiology. Nature Publishing Group, 2006.

a ( ) human → swine
b ( ) swine → human
c (X) avian → human
d ( ) swine → avian
e ( ) avian → swine

2 Read the article on page 82 again. Then answer the questions below.

2.1 When was the H1N1 flu first detected in people in the U.S.?

a (X) The H1N1 flu was first detected in people in the U.S. in June 2009.
b ( ) The H1N1 flu was first detected in people in the U.S. in April 2009.

2.2 How does this virus usually spread?

a ( ) It spreads person-to-person worldwide.
b (X) It spreads pig-to-person.

2.3 What do you understand by pandemic?

a (X) It is a disease that affects almost everyone in a very large area.
b ( ) It is a disease that is present among people living in a particular location.

3 Leia o extrato de texto abaixo e discuta-o com seus colegas.

RAFAEL GENTILE

Como você pode evitar a gripe?

Especialistas na área médica dizem que a melhor maneira de se evitar a gripe é praticar uma boa higiene. Aqui estão algumas dicas:

- lavar as mãos com água morna e sabão;
- evitar o contato com qualquer pessoa que esteja tossindo ou espirrando.

Se estiver gripado, você pode evitar a contaminação de outras pessoas:

- ficando em casa até que esteja se sentindo melhor;
- cobrindo a boca e o nariz com um lenço toda vez que tossir ou espirrar;
- lavando bem as mãos com água morna e sabão se as tiver usado para cobrir a boca ao espirrar ou tossir.

Lembre-se de que você pode espalhar a gripe por até sete dias depois de ter ficado doente, portanto, tenha cuidado mesmo depois que a maior parte dos sintomas tiver desaparecido.

[...]

Extraído de <http://saude.hsw.uol.com.br/gripe5.htm>.
Acessado em 20 de fevereiro de 2010.

a Você costuma manter hábitos preventivos no seu cotidiano?

b De que maneira você acha que a escola poderia contribuir para informar a comunidade a respeito de epidemias e formas de evitá-las?

Vocabulary in Use

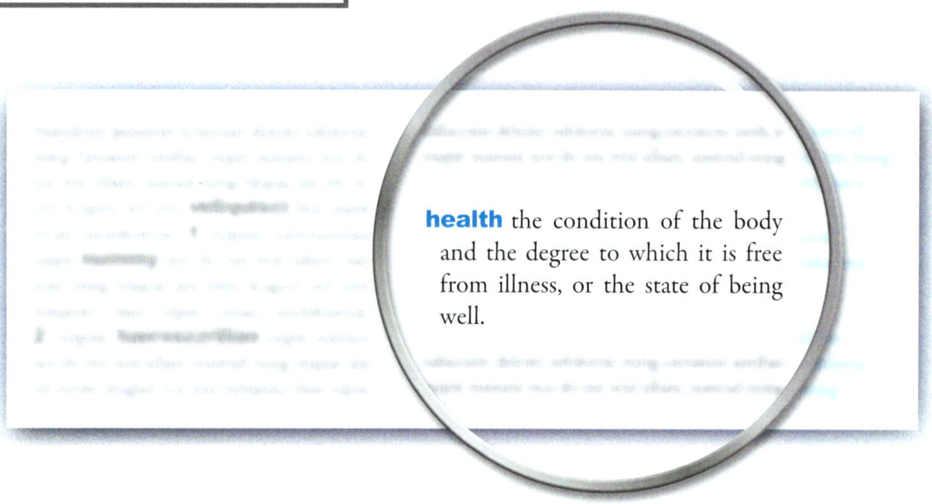

ANDREZA MOREIRA

Extracted from <http://dictionary.cambridge.org/define.asp?key=36255&dict=CALD&topic=health-in-general>.
Accessed on February 22, 2010.

In the preamble to the constitution of the World Health Organization (WHO), health is described as "a state of complete physical, mental, and social well-being and not merely the absence of disease or infirmity. [...]"

Extracted from <http://www.answers.com/topic/health>.
Accessed on February 22, 2010.

1 Read the definitions of some health problems and write the correct name for each one. Choose among the words in the box. Use the glossary if necessary.

allergy	chicken pox	depression
diabetes	diarrhea	eating disorders
gastritis	headache	otitis · ulcer

a an acute contagious disease especially of children marked by low-grade fever and formation of vesicles and caused by a herpes virus chicken pox

b a condition of general emotional dejection and withdrawal; sadness greater and more prolonged than that warranted by any objective reason depression

c an intestinal disorder characterized by abnormal frequency and fluidity of fecal evacuations diarrhea

d a sore on the skin or a mucous membrane, accompanied by the disintegration of tissue, the formation of pus, etc. Allergy

e inflammation of the ear otitis

f a condition that makes a person become ill or develop skin or breathing problems because they have eaten certain foods or been near certain substances eating disorders

g any of various disorders, as anorexia or bulimia, characterized by severe disturbances in eating habits ANOReaia

h a pain located in the head, as over the eyes, at the temples, or at the base of the skull headache

i inflammation of the stomach, especially of its mucous membrane gastritis

j any of several disorders characterized by increased urine production ulcer

2 Write the words or expressions from the box in the correct column. Use the glossary if necessary.

anxiety · arthritis · constipation · depression · insomnia · multiple sclerosis · painkillers · rest · stomachache · stress · stretching · vitamins

Emotional Problems	Physical Problems	Forms of Treatment
Auxiety	Arthitis	vitamins
depression	constipation	Rest
insonia	stomache	stretching
stress	multiple sclerosis	painkillers

Grammar in Use

PASSIVE STRUCTURES

FORMAÇÃO: **TO BE** (NO MESMO TEMPO DO VERBO PRINCIPAL) +
PARTICÍPIO PASSADO DO VERBO PRINCIPAL

This new virus (2009 H1N1) **was** first **detected** in people in the United States in April 2009.

USO

A **passive structure** é utilizada:	
• Para enfatizar a ocorrência de uma ação e não quem a executou. Assim, só mencionamos o autor da ação (agente da passiva) se for necessário ou importante.	A new road **is being built**. *Mona Lisa* **was painted** by Leonardo da Vinci.
• Em textos técnicos, científicos e reportagens.	A vaccine **has been provided**.

Nota

Em manchetes de jornais/cronologias, a voz passiva geralmente vem sem o verbo *to be*.	This new virus first detected in April 2009. (was first detected)

Quando transformamos uma frase da voz ativa para a voz passiva:
• O objeto da voz ativa torna-se o sujeito da voz passiva.
• O verbo *to be* é usado obrigatoriamente no tempo verbal principal da ativa.
• O verbo principal é usado no *Past Participle*.

Nota

Quando for mencionado quem fez a ação, usa-se *by* + o agente.	
Quando há dois objetos (um direto e um indireto), a transformação pode ocorrer de duas formas:	Ativa: He didn't send me a note. Passiva 1: I **wasn't sent** a note (by him). Passiva 2: A note **wasn't sent** to me.

1 Choose the sentence which is closest in meaning to the one given.

1.1 They will paint the doors.

a (   ) The doors will be painted.

b (   ) The doors would be painted.

1.2 I wasn't offered a drink.

a (   ) They didn't offer me a drink.

b (   ) They offered me a drink.

1.3 The teacher corrects the evaluations.

a (   ) The teacher is correcting the evaluations now.

b (   ) The evaluations are corrected by the teacher.

1.4 The plants haven't been watered.

a (   ) Somebody has watered the plants.

b (   ) Nobody has watered the plants.

1.5 New curtains should be bought.

a (   ) We need new curtains.

b (   ) We don't need new curtains.

1.6 We had taught grammar before.

a (   ) Grammar has been taught.

b (   ) Grammar had been taught.

1.7 He put the magazine back.

a (   ) The magazine was put back.

b (   ) The magazine is put back.

2 Passives are often used in songs, too. Here are extracts from famous lyrics. Match the columns.

1 I was blessed to be loved...

2 Ask her if she wants to stay a while...

3 I should have known better than to cheat a friend...

(   ) and she will be loved...
("She Will Be Loved", Maroon 5)

(   ) by someone as wonderful as you...
("Please Don't Go", K.C. & The Sunshine Band)

(   ) and waste the chance that I had been given...
("Careless Whisper", George Michael)

RAFAEL GENTILE

3 Use the passive structure in the sentences below. The first one is done for you.

ILLUSTRATIONS: MILTON RODRIGUES ALVES

a Did he type the memos?
Were the memos typed?

b They aren't watching the parade.
Are they watching the parade

c Do people speak Portuguese in Brazil?
they are speaking in portuguese

d The company has fired all the employees.
company fired the employees

e I hadn't called the plumber.
she called the plumber

4 Now use the active structure to rewrite the sentences below. The first one is done for you.

a Every year, thousands of pets are abandoned by unheartless people.
Every year, unheartless people abandon thousands of pets.

b The light bulb was invented by Thomas Edison.
____

c The museum has been visited by millions of people.
____

d The e-mails could be sent by the secretaries.
____

e Cocoa butter is made up of cocoa, chocolate, and milk.
____

5 Read the text about Seattle and fill in the blanks with the passive structure of the verbs in parentheses.

My Hometown

Many years ago, I was born in Seattle, Washington, USA. Seattle ______________ (locate) in the northwest corner of the USA. Recently, Seattle has become the focus of much international attention. Many films ______________ (make) there, probably the most famous of which is *Sleepless in Seattle* starring Meg Ryan and Tom Hanks. Seattle ______________ also ______________ (know) as the birthplace of grunge music – both Pearl Jam and Nirvana are from Seattle. For older people like myself, it ______________ (should / note) that Jimi Hendrix was born in Seattle! NBA fans know Seattle for the Seattle Supersonics which has played basketball in Seattle for more than 30 years. Unfortunately, Seattle is also famous for its bad weather. I can remember weeks and weeks of grey, wet weather when I was growing up.

Seattle has also become one of the fastest-growing business areas in the United States. Two of the most important names in the booming business scene in Seattle are Microsoft and Boeing. Microsoft ______________ (found) and ______________ (own) by the world-famous Bill Gates (how much of his software is on your computer?). Boeing has always been essential to the economic situation in Seattle. It ______________ (locate) to the north of Seattle and famous jets such as the "Jumbo" ______________ (manufacture) there for more than 50 years!

Seattle ______________ (position) between Puget Sound and the Cascade Mountains. The combination of its scenic location, thriving business conditions and exciting cultural scene makes Seattle one of America's most interesting cities.

Extracted from <http://esl.about.com/library/weekly/aa052798.htm>. Accessed on February 19, 2010.

PHOTO: DENNIS MACDONALD / ALAMY / OTHER IMAGES; ART: RAFAEL GENTILE

Reading

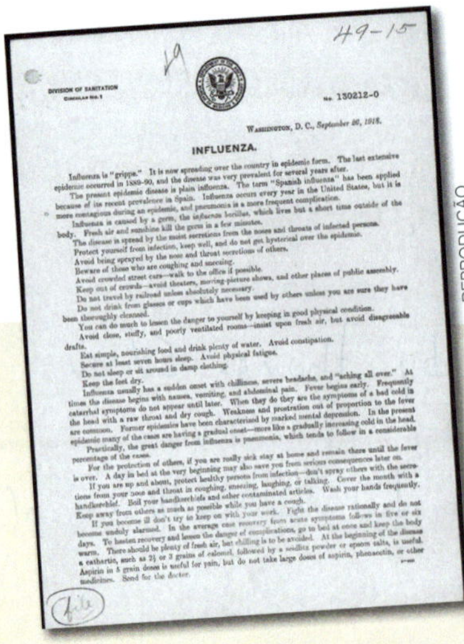

DIVISION OF SANITATION
CIRCULAR No. 1

No. 130212-0

WASHINGTON, D. C., *September 26, 1918.*

INFLUENZA

Influenza is "grippe". It is now spreading over the country in epidemic form. The last extensive epidemic occurred in 1889-90, and the disease was very prevalent for several years after.

The present epidemic disease is plain influenza. The term "Spanish influenza" has been applied because of its recent prevalence in Spain. Influenza occurs every year in the United States, but it is more contagious during an epidemic, and pneumonia is more frequent complication.

Influenza is caused by a germ, the *influenza bacillus*, which lives but a short time outside of the body. Fresh air and sunshine kill the germ in a few minutes.

The disease is spread by the moist secretions from the noses and throats of infected persons.

Protect yourself from infection, keep well, and do not get hysterical over the epidemic.

Avoid being sprayed by the nose and throat secretions of others.

Beware of those who are coughing and sneezing.

Avoid crowded street cars—walk to the office if possible.

Keep out of crowds—avoid theaters, moving-picture shows, and other places of public assembly.

Do not travel by railroad unless absolutely necessary.

Do not drink from glasses or cups which have been used by others unless you are sure they have been thoroughly cleaned.

You can do much to lessen the danger to yourself by keeping in good physical condition.

Avoid close, stuffy, and poorly ventilated rooms—insist upon fresh air, but avoid disagreeable drafts.

Eat simple, nourishing food and drink plenty of water. Avoid constipation.

Secure at least seven hours sleep. Avoid physical fatigue.

Do not sleep or sit around in damp clothing.

Keep the feet dry.

Influenza usually has a sudden onset with chilliness, severe headache, and "aching all over". At times the disease begins with nausea, vomiting, and abdominal pain. Fever begins early. Frequently catarrhal symptoms do not appear until later. When they do they are the symptoms of a bad cold in the head with a raw throat and dry cough. Weakness and prostration out of proportion to the fever are common. Former epidemics have been characterized by marked mental depression. In the present epidemic many of the cases are having a gradual onset-more likely a gradually increasing cold in the head.

Practically, the great danger from influenza is pneumonia, which tends to follow in a considerable percentage of the cases.

For the protection of others, if you are really sick stay at home and remain there until the fever is over. A day in bed at the very beginning may also save you from serious consequences later on.

If you are up and about, protect healthy persons from infection-don't spray others with the secretions from your nose and throat in coughing, sneezing, laughing, or talking. Cover the mouth with a handkerchief. Boil your handkerchiefs and other contaminated articles. Wash your hands frequently. Keep away from others as much as possible while you have a cough.

If you become ill don't try to keep on with your work. Fight the disease rationally and do not become unduly alarmed. In the average case recovery from acute symptoms follows in five or six days. To hasten recovery and lessen the danger of complications, go to bed at once and keep the body warm. There should be plenty of fresh air, but chilling is to be avoided. At the beginning of the disease a cathartic, such as 2 1/2 or 3 grains of calomel, followed by a seidlitz powder or epsom salts, is useful. Aspirin in 5 grain doses is useful for pain, bur do not take large doses of aspirin, phenacetin, or other medicines. Send for the doctor.

Extracted from <http://www.archives.gov/exhibits/influenza-epidemic/recods-list.html>. Accessed on January 30, 2010.

avoid: evite
beware: tome cuidado
boil: ferva
chilliness: calafrio
crowds: aglomerações de pessoas, multidões
disagreeable drafts: correntes de ar desagradáveis
former: antigas, passadas
keep on: manter
keep out: afaste-se
nourishing: nutritiva
onset: começo
plain: simples
street cars: bondes
unduly: indevidamente

After Reading

1 Skim through the text and write the lines where these aspects are mentioned.

		line(s)
a	characteristics of the disease	3 to 5
b	cause of the disease	6 and 7
c	infecting other people	8
d	ways of avoiding contamination	10 to 23
e	symptoms	24 to 29
f	preventing the infection of others	32 to 37
g	medicine to be taken	41 to 44

RAFAEL GENTILE

2 The following advice on how to avoid infection from influenza was taken from the text (published in 1918) on page 90. Do we have to follow the same recommendations nowadays? Write Yes or No.

a	Keep the feet dry.	No
b	Avoid being sprayed by the nose and throat secretions of other people.	Yes
c	Do not travel by railroad unless absolutely necessary.	Yes

RAFAEL GENTILE

d	Do not drink from glasses or cups which have been used by others unless you are sure they have been thoroughly cleaned.	yes
e	Boil your handkerchiefs and other contaminated articles.	NO
f	Wash your hands frequently.	yes
g	If you become ill don't try to keep on with your work.	yes

RAFAEL GENTILE

3 Os textos das páginas 82 e 90 são textos informativos, pois apresentam as seguintes características comuns a esse gênero textual: comprometimento com a realidade, narrativa estruturada em fatos e pontuação objetiva.

a Em qual dos textos os fatos são passados de forma mais didática? Fundamente sua resposta.

DA pág 82

b Qual texto apresenta sua estrutura predominantemente baseada em fatos científicos?

DA pág 90

c Sabendo que o texto informativo é baseado em fatos, por que você acha que os textos apresentam pontuação mais objetiva?

____

d Observe as datas apresentadas nos textos. Indique-as e relacione o fato principal apresentado em cada um deles.

Janeiro de 2010. pela OMS

Setembro de 1918. pela MARINHA AMERICANA

Appendix 6 page 157

Consultando outras fontes

filmes: *Ensaio sobre a cegueira* (Brasil/Canadá/Japão, 2008; direção: Fernando Meirelles)
Os doze macacos (EUA, 1995; direção: Terry Gilliam)

livros: *Meio ambiente e epidemias* (Senac Editora; Série Meio Ambiente)
A história e suas epidemias – A convivência do homem com os micro-organismos (Senac Editora; autora: Stefan Cunha Ujvari)

Health Manager

1

2

Health has become an increasingly important issue. You can't go a single day without hearing something new about health care – a new diet, a new treatment, new technologies...

There is a professional who also cares a whole lot about health. Meet the health manager.

Health managers participate in planning, controlling, and analyzing the implementation of public health policies. They are also in charge of previewing and providing the materials used in health care. Furthermore, health managers work with human resources in companies and are supposed to do some strategic planning as well.

If you decide to become a health manager, there are many places where you can work, including hospitals, health care units in general, laboratories, etc. – basically, any place where people's health is the number-one priority.

In order to be a health manager, a person has to take a course that varies from twelve hundred to sixteen hundred hours, depending on the school he or she goes to.

Based on <http://catalogonct.mec.gov.br/et_ambiente_saude_seguranca/t_gerencia_saude.php>; <www.cefetbambui.edu.br/portal/tecnico-em-gerencia-de-saude>; <www.uatlantica.pt/cursos/licenciaturas/gestao-em-saude.html>; <http://education-portal.com/search/quicksearch.html>. Accessed on February 2, 2010.

a whole lot: muito
furthermore: além disso
in charge of: responsáveis por
issue: assunto
nowadays: atualmente, hoje em dia
number-one priority: prioridade zero
twelve hundred to sixteen hundred hours: 1.200 a 1.600 horas

Você gostaria de ser técnico em gerência em saúde? Por quê? / Por que não?

Additional Practice

For exercises 1 to 9, choose the best alternative.

1 "While doctors are prescribing expensive drugs that can have devastating side effects to slow the progress of Alzheimer's, new research shows it might be possible to prevent the ________ of this cruel disease by something as simple, inexpensive, and safe as a dose of marine oil every day during our younger years. [...]"

Extracted from <http://www.naturalnews.com/028126_marine_oil_Alzheimers.html>. Accessed on January 24, 2010.

a ( ) unduly
b ( ) underway
c ( ) throughout
d ( ) moist
e ( ) onset

2 "[...] The ICMR SOFPUC study also reported a higher ________ of the illness in urban slums, in those living alone, in those with no schooling, and in those who are unemployed. Males were also reported to have had higher rate of illness. [...]"

Extracted from <http://www.inwent.org/ez/articles/087263/index.en.shtml>. Accessed on January 23, 2010.

a ( ) illness
b ( ) crowd
c ( ) sneezing
d ( ) underway
e ( ) prevalence

3 I had an allergic reaction to seafood in the middle of my trip to the Bahamas and I had to spend 2 weeks in a ________ hospital room because the air conditioning system was being replaced. That's bad luck!

a ( ) stuffy
b ( ) unduly
c ( ) handkerchief
d ( ) moist
e ( ) crowd

4 "And how many hours a day did you do lessons?" said Alice, in a hurry to change the subject.

"Ten hours the first day," said the Mock Turtle, "nine the next, and so on."
"What a curious plan!" exclaimed Alice.
"That's the reason they're called lessons," the Gryphon remarked, "because they ________ from day to day."

Extracted from CARROL, Lewis. *Alice's Adventures in Wonderland*. New York: Sterling Publishing Co., Inc, 2005. p. 88.

a ( ) sneezing
b ( ) stuffy
c ( ) crowd
d ( ) cleansed
e ( ) lessen

5 **Dr. Herowitz:** The world leaders got together last week to announce a series of investments to stop the spread of the new flu virus.

Dr. Spitz: That's good news.

Dr. Herowitz: They hope a solution to the pandemic ________ by the end of the year.

a ( ) will found
b ( ) are found
c ( ) to be found
d ( ) will have been found
e ( ) have been found

6 The president spoke to the nation this morning and affirmed that the imminent pandemic ________ and that those who suffer ________ .

a ( ) will be cured, will be avoided
b ( ) will be avoided, will be cured
c ( ) is avoided, are cured
d ( ) will avoid, will cure
e ( ) had been avoided, are cured

7 Despite all the investments in research and tests, relatively few biotechnological drugs ________.

a (X) had been approved
b (   ) had been approving
c (   ) is approved
d (   ) will approve
e (   ) is being approved

8 The housekeeper came forward, and told them it was a picture of a young gentleman, the son of her late master's steward, who ________ by him at his own expense. "He is now gone into the army," she added; "but I am afraid he has turned out very wild."

Extracted from AUSTEN, Jane. *Pride and Prejudice*. London: H. G. Clarke and Co., 1844. p. 72.

a (   ) brought up
b (   ) been brought up
c (   ) have been brought up
d (   ) had brought up
e (X) had been brought up

9 The police reported that the victims had died because of severe adverse reactions to the vaccines which ________ earlier that day.

a (   ) was administered
b (   ) will be administered
c (X) had been administered
d (   ) are being administered
e (   ) administered

10 Complete part of the lyrics of "That's Why I Love You", by Boyz II Men.

"When I'm crying you are my ________
And when it feels like I'm dying
You bring me up with just one kiss"

a (   ) damp
b (   ) stuffy
c (   ) draft wind
d (   ) onset
e (X) handkerchief

Refletindo sobre sua aprendizagem

Ao final desta unidade, você já é capaz de:

- Relacionar texto escrito com texto visual e depreender informações. ☐
- Inferir sobre o significado de pandemia. ☐
- Colocar-se como agente transformador para a comunidade em que vive. ☐
- Associar algumas doenças às suas definições. ☐
- Distinguir problemas de ordem emocional dos de ordem física e alguns tratamentos. ☐
- Reconhecer e utilizar a voz passiva em diferentes situações comunicativas, às vezes destacando o agente da passiva. ☐
- Localizar informações específicas em textos. ☐
- Relacionar informações sobre formas de contágio e prevenção da gripe em épocas diferentes. ☐
- Reconhecer algumas características inerentes aos textos informativos, sejam antigos ou atuais. ☐

Aprimorando sua aprendizagem

- Peça ajuda ao professor ou aos colegas para que esclareçam suas dúvidas.
- Refaça os exercícios.
- Visite a biblioteca da sua escola ou uma biblioteca pública e consulte livros de gramática e/ou faça leituras de seu interesse.
- Assista a filmes em inglês.

Language in Action 3

1 What do you do to keep healthy? Complete this checklist.

	often	sometimes	never
drink coffee			
drink soda			
eat junk food			
eat fresh fruit			
eat fresh vegetables			
eat candy			
miss meals			
take vitamins			
exercise			
sleep less than 8 hours a day			
get medical check-ups			

RAFAEL GENTILE

Are there any habits you would like to change?

2 Below you will find different medical problems. What do you do when you have these problems? Talk to a classmate.

- a headache
- the flu
- food poisoning
- a cut finger
- hiccups
- a mosquito bite
- stomachache
- travel sickness

RAFAEL GENTILE

3 Listen to two dialogues in which people are talking about their health problems. What are the problems mentioned? What do the friends suggest?

4

Angela	
Ben	

Writing

Imagine you are traveling to a very hot place on your holidays. What should you do to avoid getting ill while you are there? Complete the sentences below.

If I get sick on the car/bus/plane, I take some medicine.

I can avoid insect bites by using some insect protective cream.

I'm going to drink water.

I'm not going to eat junk food.

If the day is hot, I'll keep out of the sun between morning and the end of the afternoon.

What else should you do? Write your answer.

Put some Hat, to protect me from the sun

7 People with Special Needs

PRE-READING

Where was this article published? When was it published?

RAFAEL GENTILE

News | **Guardian** | Tuesday, April 12, 2005

We Can Fend for Ourselves – DPI Head

Valdeen Shears – Neptune

PRESIDENT of the local chapter of Disabled Peoples International, George Daniel, has said that his group will not allow able-bodied people to represent it in future.

"No organisation dominated by able-bodied people can represent or speak for the disabled community," he said at a news conference held at DPI headquarters on Wrightson Road, Port-of-Spain, yesterday.

Daniel's comments echoed those of representatives of other organisations.

About two weeks ago, a group called the Consortium for the Empowerment of Persons with Disabilities declared itself the umbrella organisation for the disabled community.

Daniel said this group was made up of at least ten separate organisations, but all were operated and managed by able-bodied people.

He said this move was made without either consultation or sanctioning by any member of the disabled community.

Daniel compared this with "an organisation established for women or women's rights, but run and controlled by men."

"This is basically what we are looking at," he said.

Carlos Green, president of Persons Associated with Visual Impairment, used a personal experience to deliver his point.

"As a blind person I was made to believe by the wider society that I could do nothing more than make baskets," he said.

"Through an international organisation run by a disabled person I discovered that the blind (are) capable of much, much more."

Merle Khoza, president of Disabled Women's Network, supported Green, saying disabled people were the best to articulate the issues facing them.

"Who better to say this than the disabled persons themselves?" she asked.

Extracted from <http://library2.nalis.gov.tt/infofiles/collect/news3/index/assoc/HASH01ea/240dd8f5.dir/709.jpg>. Accessed on February 11, 2010.

able-bodied: fisicamente capaz
chapter: divisão
disabled: pessoas com necessidades especiais
echoed: ecoaram
empowerment: autorização
fend for: arranjar-se, prover a própria subsistência
headquarters: sede
held: ocorrida
run: administrada
supported: apoiou
umbrella: protetora
wider: vasta, maioria

After Reading

1 Connect the sentences below to the corresponding paragraphs in the previous text.

a Carlos Green says that people wanted him to believe that he couldn't do anything really important.

10

b Things that George Daniel said reflected what other organizations also believed.

3

c There is a group that considers itself the main group for disabled people.

4

d Merle Khoza questioned if any group is more capable of discussing disabled people's needs than disabled people themselves.

13

2 Check the best alternative.

2.1 What does Daniel mean by "an organisation established for women or women's rights, but run and controlled by men"?

- **a** (X) One can only understand and support others' needs when one faces the same needs.
- **b** (   ) Solidarity is enough to help disable people.

2.2 According to Carlos Green's opinion, we can infer that:

- **a** (X) society limits the empowerment of disabled people.
- **b** (   ) society offers disabled people every resource to develop their capacities.

2.3 Merle Khoza agreed with Carlos Green's point of view because:

- **a** (   ) there are many unemployed disabled people in the U.S.
- **b** (X) it reflects the reality of disabled people.

2.4 After reading the text, we can infer that:

- **a** (X) some organizations are very important to minorities because they represent the minorities' rights and demands.
- **b** (   ) minorities don't need organizations to represent them at all.

3 Leia o texto abaixo e discuta-o com seus colegas.

RAFAEL GENTILE

Lei Federal nº 8.213, de 24 de julho de 1991, regulamentada pelo Decreto Federal 3.298, de 20 de dezembro de 1999, determina que toda empresa com mais de 100 empregados está obrigada a preencher de 2% a 5% de seus cargos com beneficiários reabilitados ou pessoas com deficiência, habilitadas, na seguinte proporção:

I. 100 até 200 empregados: 2%
II. de 200 a 500 empregados: 3%
III. de 501 a 1.000 empregados: 4%
IV. de 1.001 em diante: 5%

Extraído de <http://www.pmpf.rs.gov.br/files/cotas_no_mercado_trabalho_dir4.pdf>. Acessado em 25 de fevereiro de 2010.

a Você acha que a lei acima contribui de forma efetiva para que as pessoas com necessidades especiais tenham igualdade de condições no mercado de trabalho? Por quê?

b Você tem conhecimento de alguma pessoa com necessidades especiais que tenha tido dificuldade para conseguir colocação no mercado de trabalho?

c O que mais você acha que poderia ser feito pelos governantes para proporcionar maiores condições de trabalho, locomoção e educação para as pessoas com necessidades especiais?

Vocabulary in Use

1 Check the meaning of the words in bold.

1.1 "We can **fend** for ourselves"

a ( ) surrender **b** ( ) give up **c** (X) defend

1.2 "Daniel's comments **echoed** those of representatives of other organisations."

a ( ) repeated **b** (X) differed **c** ( ) opposed

1.3 "[...] 'an organisation established for women or women's rights, but **run** and controlled by men'."

a ( ) moved fast **b** ( ) served **c** ( ) managed

1.4 "[...] I was **made** to believe by the wider society that [...]"

a ( ) discouraged **b** ( ) induced **c** ( ) built

2 Read the sentence below, which has been extracted from the text, and pay special attention to the expression in bold.

"[...] but all were operated and managed by **able-bodied** people."

Able-bodied is a compound adjective, i.e., a combination of words that works as a single adjective. As a general rule, compound adjectives are hyphenated when they come before nouns. How do you form a compound adjective? Here are some examples:

noun + past participle	→	a hand-made toy
noun + participle *-ing*	→	a heart-breaking story
adjective + noun *-ed*	→	an able-bodied person
adverb + past participle	→	strongly built

Now, add the words in the box to the words below to form compound adjectives that describe people. Then translate the adjectives formed.

blue left level middle soft strong thick tone

a	Middle	+	-aged	=	
b	tone	+	-deaf	=	
c	Soft	+	-hearted	=	Soft-hearted
d	Strong	+	-headed	=	Strong-headed
e	left	+	-handed	=	
f	thick	+	-skinned	=	
g	level	+	-willed	=	
h	blue	+	-eyed	=	blue-eyed

3 Now choose three compound adjectives from exercise 2 and write true sentences about you, your friends, or your family members.

___

___

___

Grammar in Use

INFINITIVE AND GERUND FORMS

INFINITIVE

FORMAÇÃO: **TO** + VERBO

USO	
George Daniel has said that his group will not allow able-bodied people **to represent** DPI in the future. He also told us **not to look down on** the disabled. Merle Khoza said disabled people were the best **to articulate** the issues facing them.	
O infinitivo com **to** pode ser usado como sujeito da oração:	To combat discrimination is to understand the issues faced by disabled people.

FORMAÇÃO: VERBO SEM **TO**

USO	
É usado depois dos verbos modais (*can, may, should*), dos verbos *make* e *let* e depois de *but* e *except*.	Let me warn you about the dangers of living alone. Honesty makes me feel good. We were so touched by his life story that we did nothing but join the DPI.

GERUND

FORMAÇÃO: VERBO + **ING** (= substantivo)

USO	
Como sujeito ou objeto.	Spending all your money before Christmas wasn't a clever idea. Irresponsible Chris didn't stop smoking after she found out she was sick.
Depois de preposições.	Are you interested in improving your fluency?
Depois de alguns verbos/expressões, tais como: *appreciate, avoid, can't help, can't stand, consider, deny, enjoy, finish, keep, mind, suggest*, etc.	After listening to his sad tale, I couldn't help crying. Do you mind passing me the salt?
Verbos de percepção (*feel, hear, listen to, look at, smell, taste, touch, see, watch*) podem ser usados no gerúndio ou no infinitivo sem **to**. São usados no gerúndio quando a ação está/estava em progresso. São usados no infinitivo sem **to** quando a ação foi observada, sentida, do início ao fim.	I saw the couple dancing. (Não vi toda a dança, ela estava em progresso quando a vi.) I saw the couple dance. (Vi toda a dança do casal, do início ao fim.)

Appendix 7 page 158

1 **Choose the right infinitive form to complete the sentences.**

1.1 He promised us ________ our pets while we're away.

a ( ) to take care of **b** ( ) take care of

1.2 ________ weight Diana needs to exercise more frequently.

a ( ) To lose **b** ( ) Lose

1.3 Knock it off! Let me ________ the way I want to!

a ( ) to dress **b** ( ) dress

1.4 They can do anything except ________ my china.

a ( ) to touch **b** ( ) touch

1.5 Since Dad didn't want ________, he decided ________.

a ( ) to argue / to leave **b** ( ) argue / leave

2 **Check the correct sentences. Underline and correct the mistakes in the incorrect ones.**

a My sister goes swim on Mondays and Wednesdays. ____________________

b My friend left the party without waiting for me. ____________________

c To run is my favorite sport. ____________________

d The architect tried to solve the problem in the house, but he couldn't. ____________________

e Mark enjoys to stay at home. ____________________

f They didn't remember locking the door yesterday night. ____________________

3 **Use either the gerund or infinitive form of the verbs in parentheses to complete these famous quotations.**

a "All talk of ________________ (win) the people by ________________ (appeal) to their intelligence, of ________________ (conquer) them by impeccable syllogism, is so much moonshine."
(H. L. Mencken)

b "Eighty percent of success is ________________ (show up)."
(Woody Allen)

c "Humor is ________________ (laugh) at what you haven't got when you ought to ________________ (have) it."
(Langston Hughes)

d "________________ (feel) gratitude and not ________________ (express) it is like ________________ (wrap) a present and not ________________ (give) it."
(William A. Ward)

e "The dead might as well ______________________ (try / speak) to the living as the old to the young."
(Willa Cather)

f "O, burn her, burn her. ______________________ (hang) is too good!"
(William Shakespeare in *King Henry the Sixth*)

g Because musicians have no gold for ______________________ (sound)."
(William Shakespeare in *Romeo and Juliet*)

4 Underline the best verb form to complete the following text.

RAFAEL GENTILE

Immigrant Charter Schools: A Better Choice?

WWW.CARTOONSTOCK.COM

"Must be one of those charter schools I keep hearing about."

Third-grader Jaime of Denver, Colorado, was having a hard time concentrating in school. The son of Mexican immigrants, he had learned to speak English perfectly in his dual-language public school, but **to read / read / reading** and **to write / write / writing** was another story.

"The **to teach / teach / teaching** method wasn't working for him," said Jaime's mother, Xochitl Rico. She was anxious **to change / change / changing** schools, but, due to the economy, could not afford **to spend / spend / spending** extra money on the English **to tutor / tutor / tutoring** he would **to need / need / needing**.

"I had **to choose / choose / choosing** between **to pay / pay / paying** for health insurance and tutoring," Rico said.

A friend told her about Cesar Chavez Academy, a new tuition-free charter school where the majority of students are of Hispanic origin. [...]

"I was surprised. They are motivated and want **to be / be / being** number one in the class. My oldest is writing and reading in English. It was everything I was looking for," Rico said.

Stories like Rico's are becoming increasingly common as parents of English-language learners, or ELLs, are turning to charter schools **to provide / provide / providing** their children with a school experience that meets their academic needs and honors their cultural heritage. [...]

Extracted from <http://www.tolerance.org/magazine/number-37-spring-2010/immigrant-charter-schools-better-choice>. Accessed on March 1, 2010.

5 Match.

a I should stop eating chocolate because I'm…

b Dan stopped to pick out some flowers…

c Sorry, we didn't mean to be rude, but…

d Sponsoring…

e Does she remember paying the bill?

f Did you remember to close the windows?

( ) It'll probably rain.

( ) overweight and the doctor said it's important to count the calories.

( ) means sharing goals.

( ) on his way home.

( ) I doubt it! She's very forgetful!

( ) you weren't very polite either.

6 Read the text and write the verbs in parentheses in either the gerund or in the infinitive form.

The Equal Rights Center

Ensuring Civil Rights Are Your Rights

PHOTO: JUPITER UNLIMITED / IMAGEPLUS; ART: RAFAEL GENTILE

The Equal Rights Center (ERC) is a comprehensive non-profit civil rights organization dedicated to ____________ (identify), ____________ (challenge), and ____________ (eliminate) discrimination. With more than 25 years of ____________ (advance) civil rights, today the ERC and our thousands of members address issues of discrimination in six areas: fair housing, fair employment, disability rights, access to government services, and immigrant rights. […]

WHAT WE DO

- ____________ (Counsel) and Advocacy: […] Free and confidential counseling and advocacy. […]
- Enforcement Efforts: […] by ____________ (pursue) administrative and civil-court remedies ____________ (stop) discrimination. […]
- Testing: ____________ (identify) and ____________ (combat) discrimination, the ERC employs a recognized investigative method ____________ (assess) compliance with civil rights law. For more information on ____________ (test), or ____________ (become) a paid tester, please contact the ERC. […]

Extracted from <http://www.equalrightscenter.org/education/documents/WhatWeDo.pdf>. Accessed on March 1, 2010.

Reading

Factsheet on Persons with Disabilities

Overview

- Around 10 percent of the world's population, or 650 million people, live with a disability. They are the world's largest minority.
- This figure is increasing through population growth, medical advances and the ageing process, says the World Health Organization (WHO). [...]
- Eighty percent of persons with disabilities live in developing countries, according to the UN Development Programme (UNDP).
- Disability rates are significantly higher among groups with lower educational attainment in the countries of the Organization for Economic Cooperation and Development (OECD), says the OECD Secretariat. On average, 19 percent of less-educated people have disabilities, compared to 11 percent among the better educated. [...]
- Women with disabilities are recognized to be multiply disadvantaged, experiencing exclusion on account of their gender and their disability. [...]
- According to UNICEF, 30 percent of street youths have some kind of disability. [...]
- Comparative studies on disability legislation shows that only 45 countries have anti-discrimination and other disability-specific laws. [...]

Extracted from <http://www.un.org/disabilities/default.asp?id=18>. Accessed on February 26, 2010.

attainment: resultado
disability: deficiência
figure: imagem, forma
growth: aumento

After Reading

1 Match the columns according to the information in the text.

a Worldwide percentage of people living with some form of disability.

b Percentage of disabled people who live in developing countries.

c Percentage of disabled people among the less-educated population.

d Incidence of disability among young homeless people.

e Number of countries with legislation on disability.

(c) 19

(e) 45

(d) 30

(a) 10

(b) 80

2 "According to Unicef, 30 percent of street youths have some kind of disability."

This is an extract from the text on page 106. Read a little bit more about this issue and complete the sentences.

Adolescence is a time of great emotional and psychological change, of emerging sexuality, and important life choices about employment and education. During this period of transition adolescents, especially those with disabilities, may be vulnerable in society; their rights have not been always been recognised. Disability programmes tend to focus on young children or adults, and may risk excluding adolescents, negatively affecting their opportunities to develop their abilities and to participate in community life. Factors in disabled adolescents' development and socialisation include the attitude and behaviour of parents, family members, and peers, and social and community values. [...]

RAFAEL GENTILE

Extracted from <http://asksource.ids.ac.uk/cf/keylists/keylist2.cfm?topic=az&search=QL_DISAD05>. Accessed on March 2, 2010.

a The main changes faced by teenagers in adolescence are emotional, psychological and emerging sexuality.

b Disability programs tend not to focus on old people.

c Adolescents' development have not been recognized.

3 As características abaixo são inerentes aos textos jornalísticos. Dentre elas, assinale as que podem ser encontradas no texto da página 98.

RAFAEL GENTILE

a Apresenta título. (X)

b Apresenta o nome do jornalista autor da matéria. ( )

c Apresenta um parágrafo introdutório resumindo o assunto. ( )

d Apresenta fatos, eventos e experiências. (X)

e Apresenta o ponto de vista pessoal do jornalista. ( )

f Identifica fontes das informações. ( )

g Recapitula a matéria no parágrafo final. (X)

Consultando outras fontes

filmes: *Meu pé esquerdo* (Inglaterra/Irlanda, 1989; direção: Jim Sheridan)
A força de um campeão (Canadá, 1983; direção: Ralph Thomas)

livro: *Feliz ano velho* (Objetiva; autor: Marcelo Rubens Paiva)

Orthotists and Prosthetists

1

2
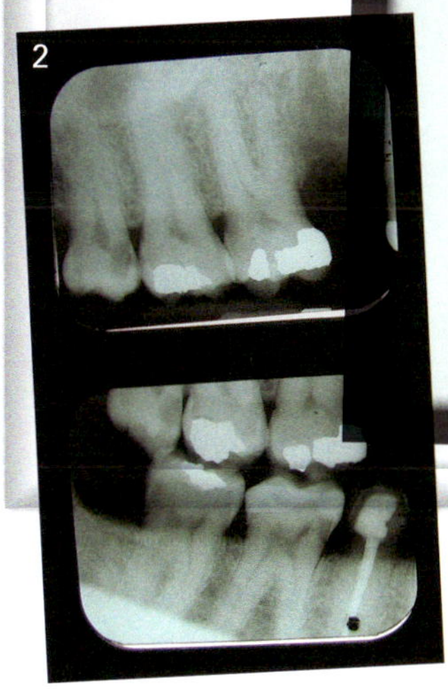

PHOTOS: 1. MAHMOUD RAOUF MAHMOUD / REUTERS / LATINSTOCK, 2. TOM GRUNDY / SHUTTERSTOCK; ART: RAFAEL GENTILE

Do you know the difference between prosthetics and orthotics? Well, I can tell you this: you would rather need the latter than the former, at any time. That's because an orthotic is a device that corrects a temporary need – such as the braces you have on your teeth, for example – and a prosthetic is an artificial replacement for a portion of the body that is missing or disfigured, which means it is made for permanent deficiencies, like your grandfather's hearing aid. Both devices are provided by an orthotic and prosthetic technician – or O and P technician, if you will.

An O and P technician is in charge of examining people who need these kinds of devices (under the supervision of a doctor), analyzing the materials they should be made of, making the orthotics and prosthetics themselves, and tending to the patients if the devices need any adaptations.

In order to provide better positioning, properly accommodate on the body, and relieve pain – thus offering as much comfort as possible – most of these devices are unique and custom-made. Some of the materials used to produce prosthetics and orthotics are fiberglass, silicone, and carbon fibers.

If you decide to be an O and P technician, you will probably work at a hospital, at an orthopedic clinic, or even at a rehabilitation center.

The course a person needs to take in order to become one of these professionals is 1200 to 1600 learning hours long, depending on the school you choose.

Based on <http://catalogonct.mec.gov.br/ct_ambiente_saude_seguranca/t_orteses_proteses.php>; <www.ceeteps.br/Cursos/ETE/Orteses_Proteses.html>; <http://diplomaguide.com/articles/Prosthetic_Technician_Career_Info.html>; <www.nhscareers.nhs.uk/details/Default.aspx?Id=286>; <www.wisegeek.com/what-are-orthotics-and-prosthetics.htm>. Accessed on March 2, 2010.

braces: aparelho (de dentes) fixo
custom-made: feitos sob medida
device: aparelho (termo genérico)
hearing aid: aparelho de surdez
if you will: se preferir
orthotic: órtese
prosthetic: prótese
relieve: aliviar
thus: assim, deste modo
would rather: preferiria

Você gostaria de ser técnico em órteses e próteses? Por quê? / Por que não?

Additional Practice

For exercises 1 to 10, choose the best alternative.

1 All the employees signed a petition asking for the installation of a ________ ramp to provide easy access to a co-worker who has mobility problems.

a ( ) disabled
b ( ) issues
c ( ) be regarded
d ( ) wheelchair
e ( ) highlight

2 "The Washington State Hospital Association is urging the state to make flu shots ________ for health-care workers – a dramatic step that the state's top health official is already rejecting as unnecessary government intrusion.
[...]"

Extracted from <http://seattletimes.nwsource.com/html/localnews/2009977314_swinevaccine01m.html>. Accessed on January 24, 2010.

a ( ) disabled
b ( ) issues
c ( ) be regarded
d ( ) wheelchair
e ( ) mandatory

3 The company decided to install many special doors and ramps because they don't want it to ________ as a company that doesn't care about its disabled employees.

a ( ) disabled
b ( ) issues
c ( ) be regarded
d ( ) wheelchair
e ( ) highlight

4 The aim of this innovative project is to ________ the importance of tolerance and non-discriminative behavior among children at a very early age in school.

a ( ) disabled
b ( ) highlight
c ( ) be regarded
d ( ) wheelchair
e ( ) issues

5 I read an article about how ________ the needs of disabled people can make us more responsive to the needs of all the population in general. It's very interesting and I never thought about it before.

a ( ) to be understood
b ( ) is understanding
c ( ) understood
d ( ) to understand
e ( ) understanding

6 In his last speech, the prime minister emphasized the importance of ________ appropriate strategies ________ with the issues of disabled people in our society.

a ( ) to develop, to deal
b ( ) developing, dealing
c ( ) developing, to deal
d ( ) to develop, dealing
e ( ) develop, deal

7 "[...]
Seller has not received any written notice from, and to Seller's knowledge there are no grounds for, any governmental agency ________ the correction of any condition with respect to the Property, or any part thereof, by reason of a violation of any applicable federal, state, county, or municipal law, code, rule, or regulation (including those ________ the Americans With Disabilities Act), which has not been cured or waived.
[...]"

Extracted from <http://www.faqs.org/sec-filings/100108/Grubb-and-Ellis-Healthcare-REIT-II-Inc_8-K/exhibit1.htm>. Accessed on January 23, 2010.

a ( ) requiring, to respect
b ( ) requiring, respecting
c ( ) to require, respecting
d ( ) require, respect
e ( ) to require, to respect

8 This organization has more than 20 years of experience in ________ with the disabled community in order ________ a more inclusive society.

a ( ) working, creating
b ( ) to work, to create
c ( ) to work, creating
d ( ) work, create
e ( ) working, to create

9 "When the boatman left him, he remained stupidly ________ on the sandy tongue, ________ before him though only ________ objects through the giddy whirls which made them seem phantasmagoria."

Extracted from HUGO, Victor. *The Hunchback of Notre Dame*. New York: Dick & Fitzgerald Publishers, 1862. p. 152.

a ( ) standing, staring, seeing
b ( ) standing, to stare, seeing
c ( ) standing, staring, to see
d ( ) to stand, staring, seeing
e ( ) to stand, to stare, to see

10 "[...]
Dr. Price wanted ________ a way to reassure, inform, inspire, and empower his patients who were considering surgery on their eyes ________ USABA athlete, Trischa Zorn – the most decorated Paralympic athlete in the history of disabled sport, said Mark Lucas, USABA Executive Director [...]".

Extracted from <http://cate.ca.gov/index.cfm?a=Resources&p=News&article=555>. Accessed on January 23, 2010.

a ( ) to find, to include
b ( ) finding, including
c ( ) to find, including
d ( ) find, including
e ( ) find, include

Refletindo sobre sua aprendizagem

Ao final desta unidade, você já é capaz de:

- Localizar informações específicas em textos. ☐
- Fazer inferências como estratégia de leitura. ☐
- Refletir e posicionar-se a respeito das necessidades e condições de vida social das pessoas com necessidades especiais. ☐
- Relacionar aos seus sinônimos palavras que tenham relação tema da unidade. ☐
- Formar e utilizar alguns adjetivos compostos em diferentes contextos. ☐
- Utilizar adequadamente as formas nominais de gerúndio e infinitivo e seu uso em diversas situações comunicativas. ☐
- Localizar informações numéricas em textos e associá-las a fatos. ☐
- Reconhecer e identificar características do gênero jornalístico. ☐

Aprimorando sua aprendizagem

- Peça ajuda ao professor ou aos colegas para que esclareçam suas dúvidas.
- Refaça os exercícios.
- Visite a biblioteca da sua escola ou uma biblioteca pública e consulte livros de gramática e/ou faça leituras de seu interesse.
- Assista a filmes em inglês.

8 Causes and Prevention of Obesity

PRE-READING

Look at the picture below. How can you associate the picture with the labels "calories in" and "calories out"?

Obesity

Causes and Consequences

Is there a quick answer to the question,

"What contributes to overweight and obesity?"

Overall there are a variety of factors that play a role in obesity. This makes it a complex health issue to address. This section will address how behavior, environment, and genetic factors may have an effect in causing people to be overweight and obese.

The Caloric Balance Equation

- Overweight and obesity result from an energy imbalance. This involves eating too many calories and not getting enough physical activity.
- Body weight is the result of genes, metabolism, behavior, environment, culture, and socioeconomic status.
- Behavior and environment **play a large role** causing people to be overweight and obese. These are the greatest areas for prevention and treatment actions.

Adapted from <http://www.surgeongeneral.gov/topics/obesity>.

When it comes to maintaining a healthy weight for a lifetime, the bottom line is – calories count! Weight management is all about balance – balancing the number of calories you consume with the number of calories your body uses or **burns off**.

- A **calorie** is defined as a unit of energy supplied by food. A calorie is a calorie regardless of its source. Whether you're eating carbohydrates, fats, sugars, or proteins, all of them contain calories.
- **Caloric balance** is like a scale. To remain in balance and maintain your body weight, the calories consumed (from foods) must be balanced by the calories used (in normal body functions, daily activities, and exercise).

If you are...	your caloric balance status is...
maintaining your weight	*in balance* – You are eating roughly the same number of calories that your body is using. Your weight will remain **stable**.
gaining weight	*in caloric excess* – You are eating more calories than your body is using. You will store these extra calories as fat and you'll **gain** weight.
losing weight	*in caloric deficit* – You are eating fewer calories than you are using. Your body is pulling from its fat storage cells for energy, so your weight is **decreasing**.

Genetics and the environment may increase the risk of personal weight gain. However, the choices a person makes in eating and physical activity also contribute to overweight and obesity. [...]

Extracted from <http://www.cdc.gov/obesity/causes/index.html>.
Accessed on March 2, 2010.

Appendix 8
page 159

address: lidar
body weight: peso corporal
fats: gorduras
imbalance: desequilíbrio
overall: em geral
overweight: sobrepeso
regardless of: indiferente de
roughly: aproximadamente
scale: balança
storage: armazenagem
store: armazenar
supplied: suprida

After Reading

1 After reading the text, can you quickly answer the question, *"What contributes to overweight and obesity?"*? Why? / Why not?

leak of exercises and bad alimentar habits

2 What type of combination results in body weight?

a ( ) Metabolism, good behavior, exercises, and socioeconomic imbalance.
b (X) Behavior, culture, environment, genes, metabolism, and socioeconomic status.
c ( ) Genes, and socioeconomic status.

3 What is the result of good weight management?

a ( ) Maintaining your weight in balance.
b ( ) Gaining weight with caloric excess.
c (X) Losing weight with caloric deficit.

4 Check the correct meaning of the words in bold.

4.1 "[...] the number of calories your body uses or **burns off**."
a ( ) consome b (X) queima c ( ) usa

4.2 "Behavior and environment **play a large role** [...]"
a (X) têm um papel importante
b ( ) jogam um rolo grande
c ( ) têm o papel principal

4.3 "Your weight will remain **stable**."
a ( ) instável b ( ) irregular c (X) estável

4.4 "[...] you'll **gain** weight."
a ( ) perder b (X) ganhar c ( ) eliminar

4.5 "[...] your weight is **decreasing**."
a ( ) eliminando b (X) diminuindo c ( ) perdendo

4.6 "Genetics and the environment may **increase** the risk of personal weight gain."
a (X) aumentar b ( ) diminuir c ( ) estabilizar

5 Leia o texto abaixo e discuta-o com seus colegas.

> [...] Embora a concentração de renda no Brasil (as classes de renda mais baixa utilizam 37% da renda com alimentação e as mais altas empenham 11%) não permita falar em mercado homogêneo, nas duas últimas décadas houve um predomínio no consumo de alimentos industrializados comprados em supermercados em todas as classes de renda.
>
> Hoje, nos supermercados da maioria das cidades brasileiras, é possível adquirir alimentos resfriados, congelados, temperados, preparados, empanados, recheados, em forma de hambúrguer, almôndegas etc., e a maior parte dos produtos tem como indicação de cozimento a fritura. Dessa forma, o aumento da concentração energética pode se dar pelos recheios, molhos, temperos acrescentados aos produtos e pelo modo de preparo. [...]

RAFAEL GENTILE

Extraído de <http://www.efdeportes.com/efd121/obesidade-na-adolescencia.htm>.
Acessado em 2 de março de 2010.

a Por que o consumo de alimentos industrializados vem aumentando nas últimas décadas?

b Você e sua família têm o hábito de sentar-se à mesa para as refeições? A comida é preparada em casa?

c Você se preocupa com sua alimentação? Como?

Vocabulary in Use

1 If you go back to the text on page 112, you will find the following sentence:

> "This section will address how behavior, environment, and genetic factors may have an effect in causing people to be **overweight** and **obese**."

As you can see, there are different ways to describe a person who is fat. We usually use the word fat to talk about ourselves. It is rude to say someone else is fat. It is more polite to say that they are large or overweight, for example.

Use the adjectives in the boxes to complete the sentences on page 115. Use the glossary if necessary.

chubby | **fat** | **large** | **plump** | **overweight** | **obese**

RAFAEL GENTILE

a Do I look __________ in this sweater?

b Many teenagers in Brazil are __________ because they don't get enough exercise.

c Her daughter is a small and __________ girl.

d Who is that __________ little boy with dark hair?

e I was afraid because I was stopped by two __________ men on the street when I was coming back to school.

f Doctors have recommended that new diet as a treatment for the __________ women on the island.

2 **Some people exercise because they want to lose weight. Others exercise because they simply like it. Below you will find some words or expressions related to exercising. Match these expressions to their definitions.**

a exercises
b get some exercise
c exercise
d exercise class
e join a gym
f get into shape
g lose weight
h sports center
i work out

2.1 building where you can do lots of different types of sport as well as exercise classes and weight training ( )

2.2 a class where a group of people do exercises ( )

2.3 do exercise when you do not usually do any ( )

2.4 pay money to a gym so that you can go there and use it whenever you want ( )

2.5 exercise to get in shape and reduce stress ( )

2.6 to become thinner ( )

2.7 to do sports, swim, etc., in order to stay healthy and become stronger ( )

2.8 to exercise in a gym or in a class using all of the important muscles in your body, especially when you do this regularly ( )

2.9 particular movements that you repeat many times to make a part of your body stronger ( )

Grammar in Use

VERB TENSE REVIEW

Tempo verbal	Formação	Uso	Expressões	Exemplos
Simple Future	*Will* + verbo no infinitivo sem a partícula *to*	Ações ou previsões quanto ao futuro; pedido	tomorrow, tonight, next..., in...	She **will sleep** early tomorrow.
Future Continuous	*Will be* + verbo + *ing*	Ações que estarão ocorrendo em um determinado tempo no futuro	tomorrow, tonight, next..., in...	She **will be sleeping** in 2 hours.
Present Perfect	*Have/has* + particípio passado do verbo principal	Ações que aconteceram em um passado indefinido	since, for, just, ever, never, already, yet, lately, recently, many times	She **has slept** early lately.
Present Perfect Continuous	*Have/has been* + verbo principal + *ing*	Ação iniciada no passado e que ainda está em progresso por um período de tempo específico	how long, since, for, lately	She **has been sleeping** early since March.
Past Perfect	*Had* + particípio passado do verbo principal	Ação no passado que acontece antes de uma outra ação também no passado	when, after, before, already	She **had** already **slept** when I called her.
Past Perfect Continuous	*Had been* + verbo principal + *ing*	Uma ação que estava acontecendo no passado antes de uma outra ação também no passado	when, after, before, already	She **had been sleeping** for hours when I called her.
Future Perfect	*Will* + *have* + particípio passado do verbo principal	Ação que terá (ou não) acontecido antes de um determinado momento no futuro	by	She **will have slept** by the time I call her.

1 Circle the verb forms and match the pictures to the descriptions.

a Richard gained weight because he had been overeating.

b The little boy will be watching TV all afternoon.

c The woman has been cooking for hours.

d The flight attendant will have flown around the world by the time she retires.

e She has written five letters.

f After he had stepped on a banana peel, he slipped.

g The boys will fly their kites until it starts raining.

ILLUSTRATIONS: MILTON RODRIGUES ALVES

2 Match.

a She hadn't been using the seat belt…
b Will they be bike riding…
c Tony will have spent all his salary…
d We had had our lunch…
e The reporter will interview the players…
f I haven't gone skating…
g How long has she been…

( ) before Mom did the dishes.
( ) when the accident happened.
( ) at this time tomorrow?
( ) since I was 10.
( ) wearing her leather coat?
( ) by the end of the month.
( ) next season.

3 Supply the correct verb tense of the verbs in parentheses.

a Tonight I _____________ (ask) her for money because I'm broke.

b The students _____________ (neg. – memorize) all the verbs when the teacher came back from the break.

c By the time the gas station attendant finally came to fill up the tank, we _____________ already _____________ (decide) not to wait for him any longer.

d Tomorrow we _____________ (proceed) with the grammar explanation.

e The troops _____________ (march) since early this morning. Isn't it time for them to rest?

f My parents _____________ always _____________ (be) nice people.

g We swear that we _____________ (solve) all our money issues by the end of the week.

h He _____________ (wait) for us when our train arrives. I am sure he _____________ (stand) on the platform when we pull into the station.

i She _____________ (talk) for over an hour before Claire arrived.

j We _____________ (watch) TV when she arrives tonight.

k I _____________ (neg. – study) Chinese very long.

l _____________ they _____________ (see) that play many times?

m I _____________ (help) her later.

4 Read these two letters from teens in trouble and choose the appropriate verb form to fill in the blanks.

RAFAEL GENTILE

Letters

I am very sad. I ____________ already ____________ (have… tried / will… have tried) to improve, but I have failed. My problem is that I am not bright. The doctors ____________ (have diagnosed / have been diagnosing) me as normal but I'm sure I ____________ (will flunk / will have flunked) at least 5 subjects by the end of this semester, although I ____________ (have been studying / had been studying) really hard. I ____________ never really ____________ (have… succeeded / had… succeeded). I am older than most of the others in my class. The other students in my class ____________ (have been managing / had managed) to pass even before the finals but in my case, I ____________ probably ____________ (have… attended / will… be attending) this same grade next year.

(*Student in despair*)

I am 16 years old and the only child of my parents. My problem is that they don't let me go out anywhere. My prom ____________ (has been / will be) next week and they ____________ (won't let / haven't let) me attend. I ____________ never ____________ (will… go / have… gone) to parties and movies like other people of my age. I wonder if my folks ____________ (have become / will have become) less strict by the time I turn 20! It ____________ (hasn't been / hadn't been) a problem before I realized how long I ____________ (will miss / have been missing) so much fun!

(*Unhappy daughter*)

Reading

File Edit View Favorites Tools Help

Address http://www.mayoclinic.com/health/obesity/DS00314/DSECTION=prevention Go Links »

Obesity

Prevention

By Mayo Clinic staff

Whether you're at risk of becoming obese, currently overweight, or at a healthy weight, you can take steps to prevent unhealthy weight gain and related health problems. Not surprisingly, the steps to prevent weight gain are the same as the steps to lose weight: daily exercise, a healthy diet, and a long-term commitment to watch what you eat and drink.

- **Exercise regularly.** One of the most important things you can do to prevent weight gain is to exercise regularly. According to the American College of Sports Medicine, you need to get 150 to 250 minutes of moderate-intensity activity per week to prevent weight gain. Moderately intense physical activities include fast walking and swimming.
- **Eat healthy meals and snacks.** Focus on low-calorie, nutrient-dense foods, such as fruits, vegetables, and whole grains. Avoid saturated fat and limit sweets and alcohol. Remember that no one food offers all the nutrients you need. Choose a variety of foods throughout the day. You can still enjoy small amounts of high-fat, high-calorie foods as an infrequent treat. Just be sure to choose foods that promote a healthy weight and good health more often than you choose foods that don't.
- **Know and avoid the food traps that cause you to eat.** Identify situations that trigger out-of-control eating. Try keeping a journal and write down what you eat, how much you eat, when you eat, how you're feeling, and how hungry you are. After a while, you should see patterns emerge. You can plan ahead and develop strategies for handling these types of situations and stay in control of your eating behaviors.
- **Monitor your weight regularly.** People who weigh themselves at least once a week are more successful in keeping off excess pounds. Monitoring your weight can tell you whether your efforts are working and can help you detect small weight gains before they become big problems.
- **Be consistent.** Sticking to your healthy-weight plan during the week, on the weekends, and amidst vacation and holidays as much as possible increases your chances of long-term success.

If you really want to prevent weight gain, the best approach is to focus on an active lifestyle that includes an eating plan that's enjoyable, yet healthy and low in calories.

Start

Extracted from <http://www.mayoclinic.com/health/obesity/DS00314/DSECTION=prevention>. Accessed on March 3, 2010.

amidst: entre
approach: caminho, abordagem
currently: neste momento
emerge: surgirem
journal: diário, registro
patterns: ações que se repetem
traps: armadilhas
trigger out: causar, desencadear
weight gain: aumento de peso
whether: se

After Reading

1 Check the best alternatives, according to the text. More than one answer is possible.

1.1 Steps in the prevention of obesity mentioned in the text:

a (X) a healthy diet
b ( ) regular intake of tranquilizers
c ( ) liposuction
d ( ) persistence
e ( ) physical activities

1.2 In relation to exercise, the article recommends:

a ( ) intense activity once a week.
b (X) regular, moderate-intensity activity.
c ( ) daily exercise sessions of 150 minutes.
d ( ) activities like fast-walking and swimming.
e ( ) intense activity every day.

1.3 Recommended diet:

a (X) prefer low-calorie foods
b ( ) eliminate high-calories completely
c ( ) focus on one kind of nutrient
d ( ) never consume any sweets or alcohol
e ( ) focus on fruits, vegetables, and whole grains

1.4 In order to control what you eat, you should:

a ( ) write to a friend telling them everything you eat.
b ( ) only eat something when you feel very hungry.
c ( ) keep a record of what you eat.
d (X) learn to recognize and deal with situations that make you eat without control.
e ( ) weigh yourself at least once a week.

2 Circle the words or phrases that do not belong in each group.

RAFAEL GENTILE

a weight gain
lose weight
overweight
obesity
effort

b diet
health
calories
nutrient
low-fat

c fast walking
exercise
physical activity
aerobics
moderate

d be sure
avoid saturated fat
prevent weight gain
keep a healthy diet
exercise daily

3 O texto análise tem por objetivo informar ao leitor a respeito de um determinado assunto sob um ponto de vista técnico. Volte aos textos das páginas 112 e 120 responda às questões abaixo.

a A introdução do texto de abertura é baseada em quais fatos?

Em fatos cientificos e comprovados

b No texto da página 120 há um parágrafo de conclusão? E no primeiro texto?

Sim. no primeiro texto não

c Por que podemos afirmar que ambos os textos foram escritos sob o ponto de vista técnico?

Por que tinham informações baseadas em fatos e pesquisas

Consultando outras fontes

filmes: *O amor é cego* (EUA, 2001; direção: Peter Farrely e Bobby Farrely)
Super Size Me (EUA, 2004; direção: Morgan Spurlock)

livro: *Obesidade: prevenindo e controlando a epidemia global* (Roca; Organização Mundial da Saúde)

PHOTO: IOFOTO / SHUTTERSTOCK; ART: RAFAEL GENTILE

Physician

The human body is a machine that works perfectly most of the time. All of your cells work together in order to keep your machine running for as long as you live. But what if they fail? Well, that is when the doctor comes in.

A physician – also known as doctor – is the professional whose job is to maintain or restore human health by studying, diagnosing, and treating diseases or injuries. The road to becoming a doctor, however, is quite long. After taking a test, you get into college, where you'll be spending the next six years of your life studying a variety of disciplines that concern the human body (anatomy and pathology, for example).

After those six years, you may move on to the next step: residency, which is a stage of graduate medical training. Basically, this means that for up to four years you'll be practicing medicine, but always under the supervision of a doctor.

Then, if you want to specialize in a certain area of medicine, there are many different courses you can take.

One of the many specialties available is endocrinology. Endocrinologists take care of anything related to hormones. Most of the time they deal with diabetes and obesity, though any hormonal alteration is reason enough to look for an endocrinologist.

Based on <http://www.unifesp.br/dmed/dmed50.htm>;
<http://www.fmrp.usp.br/cg/novo/index.php?option=com_content&view=article&id=85&Itemid=84>;
<http://www3.pucsp.br/medicina>; <http://www.bls.gov/oco/ocos074.htm>.
Accessed on March 2, 2010.

comes in: entra, aparece
diagnosing: diagnosticando
diseases: doenças
fail: falhar, deixar de funcionar
injuries: ferimentos, lesões
reason enough: motivo suficiente
residency: residência (médica)
restore: recuperar

Você gostaria de ser médico? Por quê? / Por que não?
Você gostaria de ser endocrinologista? Por quê? / Por que não?

Additional Practice

For exercises 1 to 8, choose the best alternative.

1 If I ________ a bricklayer I'd still ________ a journeyman. – Fred L. Turner

a ( ) have been, have been
b ( ) am, were
c ( ) be, be
d ( ) had been, have been
e ( ) had been, had been

2 **Luke:** I was invited to volunteer to test this new flu shot. Do you think I should accept?

Mariah: Well, if you ________ a healthy diet, you ________ as a good candidate for the experiment.

a ( ) will have, qualify
b ( ) have, would qualify
c ( ) have, qualify
d ( ) had, qualified
e ( ) had had, will qualify

3 "At the termination of this interview, Benjamin wandered dismally upstairs and stared at himself in the mirror. He had not shaved for three months, but he ________ nothing on his face but a faint white down with which it seemed unnecessary to meddle."

Extracted from FITZGERALD, Francis Scott. "The Curious Case of Benjamin Button". In *Colliers Magazine*, May 27, 1922.

a ( ) can't find
b ( ) could
c ( ) might find
d ( ) could find
e ( ) may find

4 With the development of new technologies and tests, many beliefs we have about nutrition ________ by the end of this decade.

a ( ) will be changing
b ( ) have changed
c ( ) will have been
d ( ) have been changing
e ( ) will have changed

5 Nutritional labels ________ in the United States since the early 1990s, but they are still optional here in my country.

a ( ) have mandatory
b ( ) were mandatory
c ( ) have been mandatory
d ( ) will be mandatory
e ( ) had been mandatory

6 My father is diabetic, so I bought him this special recipe book. You know, ________ well is essential if you want ________ blood sugar.

a ( ) eating, to control
b ( ) eating, controlling
c ( ) to eat, to control
d ( ) to eat, controlling
e ( ) eat, control

7 My doctor gave me suggestions for ________ the consumption of saturated fats ________ prevent cardiovascular disease.

a ( ) reducing, help
b ( ) to reduce, help
c ( ) to reduce, to help
d ( ) reducing, to help
e ( ) reducing, helping

8 ________ through the telescope, one saw a circle of deep blue and the little round planet ________ in the field. It seemed such a little thing, so bright and small and still, faintly marked with transverse stripes, and slightly flattened from the perfect round.

Extracted from <http://www.scribd.com/doc/85771/War-of-the-Worlds-by-H-G-Wells>. Accessed on March 4, 2010

a ( ) Looking, to swim
b ( ) Looking, swimming

c ( ) To look, to swim
d ( ) Look, swimming
e ( ) To looking, to swimming

9 Complete the lyrics of "If You Leave", by Good Charlotte.

If you ________, ________ now
Please don't take my heart away
Promise me just one more night
Then we'll go our separate ways

Extracted from <http://letras.terra.com.br/omd/29415>. Accessed on March 30, 2010.

a ( ) leave, not leave
b ( ) leave, don't leave
c ( ) leaving, don't leave
d ( ) leave, might leave
e ( ) leave, don't

10 **Harold:** Did you see a nutritionist about your coffee addiction?

Jones: Yes. The nutritionist said that coffee is full of antioxidants, but I should drink it moderately from that day on.

What is the correct form of direct speech for the last sentence?

a ( ) Coffee was full of antioxidants, but you should have drunk it moderately from that day on.
b ( ) Coffee is full of antioxidants, but you should drink it moderately from now on.
c ( ) Coffee is full of antioxidants, but you should drink it moderately from that day on.
d ( ) Coffee is full of antioxidants, but I should drink it moderately from now on.
e ( ) Coffee has been full of antioxidants, but you should drink it moderately from now on.

Refletindo sobre sua aprendizagem

Ao final desta unidade, você já é capaz de:

- Fazer leitura de imagens e relacioná-las ao texto verbal. ☐
- Refletir sobre as causas da obesidade e sugestões de como evitá-la. ☐
- Descobrir o significado de palavras em inglês pelo contexto em que estão inseridas. ☐
- Discutir o aumento do consumo de produtos industrializados e como isso pode comprometer uma alimentação saudável. ☐
- Ampliar o campo semântico referente à obesidade. ☐
- Associar palavras ligadas a hábitos saudáveis às suas definições. ☐
- Reconhecer e utilizar adequadamente os tempos verbais apresentados ao longo do curso em diferentes situações comunicativas. ☐
- Sintetizar informações depreendidas de um texto. ☐
- Reconhecer palavras que não pertencem a um mesmo campo semântico. ☐
- Identificar nos textos apresentados características inerentes ao gênero análise. ☐

Aprimorando sua aprendizagem

- Peça ajuda ao professor ou aos colegas para que esclareçam suas dúvidas.
- Refaça os exercícios.
- Visite a biblioteca da sua escola ou uma biblioteca pública e consulte livros de gramática e/ou faça leituras de seu interesse.
- Assista a filmes em inglês.

Language in Action 4

1 Read the dialogue below. Then discuss the questions with a classmate.

Customer: A double cheeseburger, fries, and a soda, please.

Server: Regular or large soda?

Customer: Large, please.

Server: Anything else?

Customer: A strawberry shake.

RAFAEL GENTILE

a What's this customer's order like – healthy or unhealthy?

b What may happen to people who have this kind of diet?

c Do you think the rate of overweight or obese people in Brazil is high?

2 Are you for or against the statements below? Why? Discuss the statements in small groups.

"Overweight and obesity are defined as excessive fat accumulation that presents a risk to health."

RAFAEL GENTILE

"Overweight and obesity are major risk factors for a number of chronic diseases, including diabetes, cardiovascular diseases, and cancer."

"Implementing prevention programs and getting a better understanding of treatment for youngsters is important to control the obesity epidemic."

"Being overweight or obese may cause little or no inconvenience to a person's career."

"Weight discrimination is a very serious social problem that we need to pay attention to."

3 (5) Listen to Betty's story and fill in the blanks.

I had a beautiful ________________ when I was younger because I used to pay attention to ________________ I ate. Now I'm not ________________ ________________ ________________ I used to be. I ________________ ________________ and had two kids. Sometimes I even don't pay attention to ________________ ________________ ________________ ________________ at all.

Writing

In pairs, write a paragraph giving your opinion about the following sentence.

"Overweight people are frequently stereotyped as emotionally impaired people."

____

____

____

____

____

____

____

____

____

RAFAEL GENTILE

Cross-Curricular Activities

RIGHTS AND DUTIES

Cross-Curricular Connection: Sociology

Read the extracts below and do the activity that follows.

"All human beings are born free and equal in dignity and rights. They are endowed with reason and conscience and should act towards one another in a spirit of brotherhood."

Article 1 of the United Nations Universal Declaration of Human Rights

Extracted from <http://en.wikipedia.org/wiki/Human_rights>. Accessed on February 23, 2010.

PHOTO: HELDER ALMEIDA / SHUTTERSTOCK; ART: RAFAEL GENTILE

"When we demand our rights we should also remember our duties. We cannot isolate duty separately while asking for our rights. The two should go together and not separately."

The Imphal Free Press

Extracted from <http://www.manipuronline.com/Editorials/rightsduties.htm>. Accessed on February 23, 2010.

In groups:

- Discuss what the classroom rules should be and make a list of rights and duties.
- Exchange lists with the other groups in the classroom so that everyone can read and express their opinions.
- Once the whole class agrees with the rules, elect a class secretary to write the rules down.
- This document should be signed by all members of the classroom, including your teacher, and be respected throughout the year.

WOMEN'S RIGHTS

Cross-Curricular Connections: Sociology, Health

Take a look at the poster below and do the activity that follows.

In groups:

- Discuss the problem pictured in the poster.
- What do you think the "medicine" to cure this public health problem would be?
- Think of future changes based on your group's ideas and write headlines for a newspaper, magazine, or website to share the good news with the world.
- Show your headlines to the rest of the class.

CREATIVE WRITING

Cross-Curricular Connections: Arts, Literature

Read the poem and do the activity below.

The Cat

What a lovely cat!
Lying on its little bed
What a lovely cat!
So cute and so sad
What a lovely cat!
The best pet you have ever had.
What a lovely cat
Unfortunately, it's dead

Poem written by Patricia Martins,
a student at CAp – UFRJ

PHOTO: JUPITER UNLIMITED / IMAGEPLUS; ART: RAFAEL GENTILE

Extracted from <http://www.cap.ufrj.br/perspectiva/n5/Perspectiva_Capiana_5_web.pdf>. Accessed on February 24, 2010.

- Rhyme is a common pattern when it comes to writing poetry. Take the poem above as a model.
- Think of a verse which should be repeated throughout the poem. It should convey the central idea of the poem.
- Between every two repeated verses, insert a new verse. These inserted verses should rhyme.
- The last verse should be contrary to the readers' expectations and surprise the readers, just like the dead cat in the poem above.
- Now that your poem is ready, hand it in to your teacher. He or she will prepare your classroom's *Book of Poems*.

DISCUSSING OBESITY AT SCHOOL

Cross-Curricular Connections: Sociology, Health

Read the piece of news below and do the activity that follows.

Sunday, February 14, 2010

To Make School Food Healthy, Michelle Obama Has a Tall Order

By Ed Bruske

First lady Michelle Obama's new campaign against childhood obesity, dubbed "Let's Move," puts improvements to school food at the top of the agenda. Some 31 million children participate in federal school meal programs, Obama noted in announcing her initiative last week, "and what we don't want is a situation where parents are taking all the right steps at home – and then their kids undo all that work with salty, fatty food in the school cafeteria," she explained. "So let's move to get healthier food into our nation's schools."

PHOTO: GERALD HERBERT / AP PHOTO / IMAGEPLUS; ART: RAFAEL GENTILE

Extracted from <http://www.washingtonpost.com/wp-dyn/content/article/2010/02/11/AR2010021103894.html>. Accessed on February 24, 2010.

In small groups:

- Think of the food you're used to eating at school and decide what other healthier options you could have.
- Create a balanced menu for the school cafeteria.
- Submit this menu to the school principal.

Extra Readings

Reading 1

Rwanda
The World's First Women-Led Country

PHOTO: NICHOLAS ROBERTS / STRINGER / GETTY IMAGES; ART: RAFAEL GENTILE

Rwanda will soon become the first country in the world where female politicians outnumber male politicians. The small central African country has made huge progress since its tragic genocide in the 1990s. It can now proudly call itself a beacon of sexual equality. The ruling party coalition won 78% of seats in the election. Women took at least 44 out of a total of the 80 seats. Women may still win another three undecided seats. The head of the country's election commission stated, "It's clear women representatives will be more than 50 percent." Since the genocide, the government has encouraged women into politics. Many in Rwanda say the election results show that people are fed up with male-dominated politics. They say women will bring freshness and change to the nation.

Women's groups were quick to praise the government of President Paul Kagame for promoting such a strong gender equality program. A female voter told the BBC's *Focus on Africa* show that the new political landscape would help strengthen her country. She explained, "Men, especially in our culture, used to think that women are there to be in the house, cook food, look after the children... but the real problems of a family are known by a woman and when they do it, they help a country to get much better. [...]"

Extracted from <http://www.breakingnewsenglish.com/0809/080918-gender_equality.doc>. Accessed on January 11, 2010.

change: mudança
freshness: novidade
look after: tomar conta, cuidar
male-dominated: dominado por homens
proudly: orgulhosamente
seats: lugares na assembleia legislativa
sexual / gender equality: igualdade sexual
strengthen: fortalecer

1 What do the words in bold mean? Check the correct answer.

1.1 "[...] the first country in the world where female politicians **outnumber** male politicians [...]"

a ( ) have less numbers

b ( ) the number is not known

c ( ) are larger in number

d ( ) there are no numbers to describe

e ( ) the number is out of question

1.2 "It can now proudly call itself a **beacon** of sexual equality."

a ( ) dark

b ( ) guiding light

c ( ) meal

d ( ) excluded

e ( ) new

1.3 "The **ruling** party coalition won 78% of seats in the election."

a ( ) measurement

b ( ) illegal

c ( ) government

d ( ) regulation

e ( ) in command

1.4 "Many in Rwanda say the election results show that people are **fed up with** male-dominated politics."

a ( ) satisfied with

b ( ) angry with

c ( ) enthusiastic about

d ( ) longing for

e ( ) tired of

1.5 "A female voter told the BBC's *Focus on Africa* show that the new political **landscape** would help strengthen her country."

a ( ) environment

b ( ) ground

c ( ) surroundings

d ( ) pathway

e ( ) neighborhood

2 According to the text, are the following statements true or false?

		TRUE	FALSE
a	President Paul Kagame encouraged women to get into politics.		
b	The government started encouraging women into politics before the genocide.		
c	Until some time ago, men in Rwanda didn't want women to get involved in anything besides household chores.		
d	Women understand the troubles inside their houses.		

3 O texto informa que:

a ( ) Ruanda deverá ser o primeiro país do mundo onde o número de mulheres na política supera o número de homens.

b ( ) Em Ruanda, os homens ainda dominam a política.

c ( ) O genocídio ocorrido na década de 1990 teve como principais vítimas as mulheres de Ruanda.

d ( ) As mulheres de Ruanda não acreditam que as mudanças no cenário político do país possam trazer bons resultados.

e ( ) Ruanda é o menor país da África.

4 Assinale a alternativa que **não** está correta, de acordo com o texto.

a ( ) O total de cadeiras a preencher na última eleição em Ruanda era 80.

b ( ) *Focus on Africa* é um noticiário da rede BBC.

c ( ) Para as mulheres de Ruanda, ainda é possível conquistar a maioria das cadeiras disponíveis para esta eleição.

d ( ) As mulheres de Ruanda estão orgulhosas por terem conquistado sua igualdade.

e ( ) Os homens ruandeses acham que as mulheres são muito frescas e precisam mudar esse comportamento para obterem a maioria dos votos da nação.

5 Os pronomes **it** e **they**, sublinhados no texto, referem-se respectivamente a:

a ( ) genocídio e mulheres ruandesas.

b ( ) genocídio e homens ruandeses.

c ( ) Ruanda e mulheres ruandesas.

d ( ) Ruanda e homens ruandeses.

e ( ) progresso e homens ruandeses.

Reading 2

BULLYING IS A BIG PROBLEM

RAFAEL GENTILE

Every day thousands of teens wake up afraid to go to school. Bullying is a problem that affects millions of students of all races and classes. Bullying has everyone worried, not just the kids on its receiving end. Yet because parents, teachers, and other adults don't always see it, they may not understand how extreme bullying can get.

Bullying is when a person is picked on over and over again by an individual or group with more power, either in terms of physical strength or social standing.

Two of the main reasons people are bullied are because of appearance and social status. Bullies pick on the people they think don't fit in, maybe because of how they look, how they act (for example, kids who are shy and withdrawn), their race or religion, or because the bullies think their target may be gay or lesbian.

Some bullies attack their targets physically, which can mean anything from shoving or tripping to punching or hitting, or even sexual assault. Others use psychological control or verbal insults to put themselves in charge. For example, people in popular groups or cliques often bully people they categorize as different by excluding them or gossiping about them (psychological bullying). They may also taunt or tease their targets (verbal bullying).

Verbal bullying can also involve sending cruel instant or e-mail messages or even posting insults about a person on a website – practices that are known as cyberbullying.

[...]

Studies show that people who are abused by their peers are at risk for mental health problems, such as low self-esteem, stress, depression, or anxiety. They may also think about suicide more.

[...]

Extracted from <http://kidshealth.org/teen/school_jobs/bullying/bullies.html>.
Accessed on January 15, 2010.

cliques: pequeno grupo de pessoas pouco amistosas
fit in: enquadram-se
gossiping: fazendo fofoca
hitting: bater
peers: colegas
punching: dar socos
sexual assault: agredir, abusar sexualmente
shoving: dar empurrões
target: alvo, meta
taunt: zombar
tease: provocar, importunar
tripping: fazer tropeçar
withdrawn: retraídos(as), reservados(as)

1 Consider the two pieces of information below:

A *topic* is the subject or the *"general idea"* of a text.

A *main idea* is the *"writer's message"* about the topic.

Now read the text again and answer the questions.

1.1 What is the topic of the text?

____

1.2 What is the main idea of the text?

____

2 Read the statements.

A Bullies feel more powerful than those they pick on.

B Some bullies can verbally control their victims by defaming them via the internet.

C The way some people look may be considered unusual by bullies and bring about the bullies' inconvenient behavior.

Now check the correct alternative, according to the text.

a ( ) A and B are correct.

b ( ) B and C are incorrect.

c ( ) A, B, and C are correct.

d ( ) A and C are incorrect.

3 Check the alternative with the words that correctly replace the underlined words below.

"Bullying is when a person is <u>picked on</u> <u>over and over again</u> by an individual or group with more power, either in terms of physical <u>strength</u> or social <u>standing</u>."

a ( ) criticized; repeatedly; force; status

b ( ) punished; above; honor; reputation

c ( ) provoked; frequently; health; dismount

d ( ) instigated; seldom; indisposition; hold up

4 You can infer from the text that:

a ( ) Parents and teachers are responsible for the problem of bullying because they pretend not to see it.

b ( ) Everybody is worried about bullying because they understand how serious it is, but nobody has done anything to prevent it and that's why bullies get stronger and stronger each day.

c ( ) Because adults such as parents and teachers ignore bullying and the consequence of this behavior, the problem of bullying has not been solved yet.

d ( ) If a person who likes to dress in weird clothes is gay or lesbian, they'll be bullied twice as much.

Reading 3

PHOTO: BRENDAN MCDERMID / REUTERS / LATINSTOCK; ART: RAFAEL GENTILE

OMG! Text Messaging: an Important Part of Response

Soon after U.S. Airways Flight 1549 took off from LaGuardia Airport, Vallie Collins heard a boom and started smelling smoke. When the captain urged passengers to brace for impact, she immediately reached for her phone.

"I thought, 'OK, I'm not going to see my husband and three children again. And I just want them to know at this point, they were the number 1 thought in my mind,'" she said. She sent them a text message: "My plane is crashing." There was no time for the final three words she wanted to include: "I love you."

The crash-landing was one of few aviation accidents in which passengers were able to send frantic dispatches to loved ones before their plane went down.

After the plane came to rest in the water, Collins and all 154 others aboard were quickly rescued by ferries and emergency crews.

Larry Snodgrass, of Lake Wylie, S.C., grabbed his cell phone as the plane descended, sending a text message to his wife telling her an engine was on fire and that he loved her with all his heart.

He said his eyes were shut as the plane hit the water, and he opened them in disbelief when he realized he was still alive.

Meanwhile around the city, witnesses were recounting what they heard and saw via text message, on the SMS-blogging service Twitter, and on online photo-sharing websites. Janis Krums wrote that there was a plane in the Hudson, and he was on the ferry going to pick up people.

Krums quickly uploaded images of passengers standing on the wings of the plane bobbing in the frigid waters, waiting to be rescued. The images were picked up by The Associated Press and distributed to media outlets around the world. Hundreds of users on the photo-sharing site *Flickr* posted photos within moments of the splash landing.

A fan club on *Facebook* quickly formed for the pilot, Chesley B. Sullenberger.

After the passengers were rescued from the sinking plane, they began calling relatives. Passenger Michele Davis, 23, of Olympia, Wash., lost her phone in the crash, so she borrowed one to call her mother, Susan Dunham.

[...]

Snodgrass was one of the last people off the plane. He told *The Herald of Rock Hill* that he called his wife as he stood in shin-deep water on the wing, waiting to be rescued. She was distraught, watching television and fearing the worst after getting that text message, but all was well.

[...]

Extracted from <http://www.cellular-news.com/story/35576.php>. Accessed on January 20, 2009.

bobbing in: balouçando; subindo e descendo na água
boom: estrondo
brace: preparar-se
crashing: caindo, aterrissando de maneira que o avião sofra danos
disbelief: descrença
dispatches: mensagens
frantic: desesperado
splash: que espirra água
urged: recomendou
witnesses: testemunhas

1 Check the alternative that shows the events in chronological order.

a ( ) 1st The plane crashed.
2nd Larry Snodgrass closed his eyes.
3rd The plane started sinking.
4th Larry Snodgrass took out his cell phone.

b ( ) 1st The captain told the passengers that they were about to crash.
2nd The Associated Press took photos.
3rd Ferries and emergency crews arrived.
4th Larry Snodgrass closed his eyes.

c ( ) 1st Vallie Collins reached for her cell phone.
2nd Larry Snodgrass sent a text message to his wife.
3rd Janis Krums informed that a plane had landed on Hudson River.
4th The passengers called their relatives.

d ( ) 1st The plane went down.
2nd Passengers could smell smoke.
3rd Many photos were posted on the internet.
4th All passengers waited for help.

e ( ) 1st The plane landed on water.
2nd Janis Krums went there to try to help the survivors.
3rd Media outlets worldwide received images from The Associated Press to publicize.
4th Larry Snodgrass was surprised to realize he wasn't dead.

2 Based on the text, choose the alternative that best completes the following sentence.

"Right after being told to get ready for the impact, [...]"

a ( ) Janis Krums announced that a plane was resting in the waters of the Hudson River.

b ( ) the captain urged the passengers to brace for impact.

c ( ) Mrs. Collins couldn't think of anything else but her kids and husband.

d ( ) Michele realized she had lost her cell phone.

e ( ) witnesses reported the accident via text message, on Twitter, and on photo-sharing websites.

3 Assinale a opção que não condiz com o texto.

a ( ) "*Meanwhile*" em "*Meanwhile around the city* [...]" é o mesmo que "enquanto isso".

b ( ) "*Number 1 thought*" em " [...] *number 1 thought in my mind*" tem significado semelhante a "único pensamento".

c ( ) "*Pick up*" em "[...] *going to pick up people* [...]" significa o mesmo que "buscar".

d ( ) "*Posted*" in "[...] *users on the photo-sharing site* Flickr *posted photos* [...]" significa o mesmo que "enviar".

e ( ) "*Took off*" em "[...] *took off from LaGuardia Airport* [...]" significa o mesmo que "*departure*".

Reading 4

BRAZILIAN MOVIES, FAMOUS INTERNATIONALLY!

O AUTO DA COMPADECIDA (A DOG'S WILL)

REPRODUÇÃO

RAFAEL GENTILE

This fanciful fantasy from Brazil (which was adapted from a play that previously inspired a top-rated Brazilian TV series) follows two poor but resourceful young men, Jack the Cricket (Matheus Nachtergaele) and Chico (Selton Mello), on their adventures. Looking for work, Jack and Chico get a job at a bakery, where the mean-spirited owner feeds them food so awful that when they give it to a dog; it kills the poor animal, leading the boys to fast-talk a priest into giving the dog a funeral mass. Later on down the road, shy Chico falls in love with beautiful Rosinha, whose father is the town's wealthiest citizen. While Chico is too timid to approach her, Jack is able to fool Rosinha's boyfriend into leaving town, leaving the field open for his friend. And finally, a gang of ruthless criminals invades the town and goes on a murder spree, with Jack gunned down along many of the town's most prominent citizens.

As Chico buries his friend, Jack matches wits in the next world with the Devil (Luis Melo), persuading the Virgin Mary (Fernanda Montenegro) to put in a good word for him and his friends to Jesus. *O Auto da Compadecida* proved to be a box-office sensation in Brazil, where it has become the nation's topgrossing homegrown feature.

Extracted from <http://www.spout.com/films/O_Auto_Da_Compadecida/195225/default.aspx>. Accessed on January 11, 2010.

CENTRAL DO BRASIL (CENTRAL STATION)

REPRODUÇÃO

Heralded by critics and film fans – and rightly so – *Central Station* is the story of an unlikely friendship between the 67-year-old Dora (Fernanda Montenegro) and a 10-year-old boy Josué (Vinicius de Oliveira). Dora works as a letter writer (employed by the illiterate) in the busy Rio de Janeiro train station. Josué's mother pays Dora to write a letter to Josué's long-missing father, only to be run over by a bus moments later. Out of guilt (namely since she rarely mails the letters people pay her to write – instead laughing over them with her roommate), she takes Josué into her home and eventually on a difficult journey to a remote part of Brazil to find Josué's father.

It's a fascinating, small tale, held together by lush photography (and sadly, substantially weakened by a sorry, repetitious score). Montenegro owns the picture, her emotions fully riding the surface of the film. Worth a look, even if you don't care for foreign fare.

Extracted from <http://www.filmcritic.com/misc/emporium.nsf/reviews/Central-Station>. Accessed on January 23, 2010.

RAFAEL GENTILE

fanciful: extravagante
fool: enganar
heralded: anunciado
mass: missa
namely: a saber
run over: atropelada
ruthless: impiedoso
spree: farra

1 Ao ler o primeiro texto, pode-se concluir que Jack e Chico:

a ( ) chegam juntos ao inferno.
b ( ) não levam sua religião muito a sério.
c ( ) não têm dinheiro nem recursos.
d ( ) sentem-se culpados pela morte do cão.
e ( ) trabalham para um patrão espirituoso.

2 Quanto ao segundo texto, pode-se concluir que:

a ( ) Dora não é uma pessoa honesta.
b ( ) Dora é funcionária da Central do Brasil.
c ( ) O pai de Josué quer que o filho vá morar com ele.
d ( ) A mãe de Josué suicidou-se para não ter que ver o ex-marido.
e ( ) Dora ajuda Josué a procurar seu pai para livrar-se do fardo que é o menino.

3 According to the context of both texts, the best synonyms for the words *illiterate*, *remote*, and *lush* are, respectively:

a ( ) uncultured, detached, and merry.
b ( ) educated, slender, and merry.
c ( ) unlettered, faint, and copious.
d ( ) insensitive, far, and inebriated.
e ( ) uneducated, distant, and luxurious.

4 De acordo com o contexto dos textos-referência, qual a melhor tradução das palavras e/ou expressões sublinhadas?

4.1 "As Chico buries his friend, Jack <u>matches wits</u> in the next world with the Devil [...]"

a ( ) inicia uma competição intelectual
b ( ) propõe acordo com seu oponente
c ( ) confronta-se [com o diabo] em disputa pelo mundo.
d ( ) encontra paz
e ( ) pede que [o diabo] o tire deste mundo

4.2 "[...] Virgin Mary (Fernanda Montenegro) <u>to put in a good word for him</u> and his friends to Jesus."

a ( ) profere uma palavra boa
b ( ) falar bem dele e dos dois amigos
c ( ) fala sobre as qualidades dos dois amigos
d ( ) indica as palavras certas a serem usadas
e ( ) é carinhosa com os dois amigos

5 Marque a alternativa que aponta corretamente uma semelhança e uma diferença entre os filmes citados nos textos.

a ( ) Ambos fizeram muito sucesso no exterior, porém só um deles trata de amizade.
b ( ) Ambos estrelam a atriz Fernanda Montenegro, mas só um deles tem como assunto principal a criminalidade no Brasil.
c ( ) Ambos tratam de protagonistas muito pobres, porém só um fala sobre amizade.
d ( ) Ambos fizeram muito sucesso no exterior, mas só um tem protagonistas pobres.
e ( ) Todas as alternativas estão erradas.

6 As expressões *fast-talk* e *gun down*, no primeiro texto, e *mail*, no segundo; significam, respectivamente:

a ( ) falar rápido, balear, corresponder
b ( ) persuadir, rebaixar, enviar
c ( ) falar rápido, assassinar, enviar
d ( ) balear, enviar, persuadir
e ( ) persuadir, balear, enviar

Reading 5

"The Korubo's future is secure as long as they are left in peace."

PHOTO: FRONTPAGE / SHUTTERSTOCK; ART: RAFAEL GENTILE

Uncontacted Tribes: Making Contact

Although most invasions of uncontacted tribes' lands are prompted by the desire of loggers, oil companies, cattle ranchers, and so forth to take the tribes' lands and resources, governments sometimes try to make contact for their own reasons.

In Brazil, the Indian affairs department Funai has long had a small unit responsible for initiating contact, as a last resort, with remote peoples who are at imminent risk of an uncontrolled and possibly disastrous collision with the outside world.

One of this unit's most extraordinary contacts took place in a remote corner of Brazil's Amazon on October 15, 1996. After months of watching and waiting, a small group of Korubo Indians overcame their fear and slowly emerged from the forest to meet the Funai team.

The tension of this historic first moment was captured on film by Sydney Possuelo, the head of the Funai unit. Unlike so many other first contacts, this initial encounter was peaceful, and no Korubo died as a result.

Some years previously, this tiny group of 24 Korubo had split off from the main group and unknowingly migrated towards an area where armed loggers and colonists were invading. Fearing for their safety, the Funai team decided to make contact with them. For months the team camped by the river bank and cut trails into the forest to locate the Korubo village, hoping that their permanent presence on the river would signal their friendly intentions.

However, this small group of Korubo remains very vulnerable to violent attacks. Their natural curiosity has led some to come out of the forest to seek contact with people travelling up and down the river. Funai has set up a guard post on the river in an attempt to stop people entering the Indians' land.

The Korubo's territory lies within the Vale do Javari indigenous reserve on the border of Brazil and Peru. It is home to seven contacted peoples and about seven uncontacted Indian groups, one of the largest concentrations of isolated peoples in Brazil.

With over eight million hectares of pristine rainforest, this area has long been targeted by rubber tappers, loggers, colonists, and drug runners, who have frequently massacred the Indians. The Korubo are not afraid to retaliate and have occasionally killed invaders, signaling their desire to be left alone.

Extracted from <http://www.survivalinternational.org/uncontactedtribes/makingcontact>. Accessed on January 26, 2010.

border: fronteira
come out of: saírem
desire: desejo
overcame: superaram
pristine: pristina; fresca e limpa
prompted by: motivadas por
remains: permanece, continua
split off: separaram-se
targeted: visada

Consider these two pieces of information when doing exercises 1 and 2:

A *fact* is something you know is true.

An *opinion* is based on feelings or impressions, not facts.

1 Check the correct alternative for each of the sentences below.

		FACT	OPINION
a	The main purpose of the Funai guard post is to keep people from getting too close to the Korubo site.		
b	Funai's encounter with the Korubo was an extraordinary event.		
c	If outsiders stay away from the Korubo Indians, the tribe will not be extinguished.		
d	Korubo Indians eventually approached the Funai team.		
e	Korubo Indians were afraid of getting close to the Funai team.		
f	Not many encounters with the Korubo have been recorded.		
g	Some Korubo have tried to contact passers-by.		
h	The Korubo want to be left alone.		

2 In "The Korubo's territory <u>lies</u> within the *Vale do Javari* indigenous reserve [...]", the word *lies* could be replaced by:

a ( ) is a lie
b ( ) lies down
c ( ) is situated
d ( ) lies around
e ( ) lays

3 Qual é a única afirmação **errada** a respeito dos Korubo?

a ( ) O primeiro contato dos indígenas com os brancos foi filmado.
b ( ) Demorou para que os Korubo perdessem o medo de se aproximar dos desconhecidos.
c ( ) Há muito interesse nas riquezas naturais da área em que eles vivem, e a exploração dessas riquezas geralmente vem acompanhada de maus tratos aos índios.
d ( ) Os indígenas começaram a se aproximar porque a Funai estava tentando impedir que as pessoas adentrassem o território deles.
e ( ) Os Korubo não têm medo de matar os que não respeitam seu desejo de ficarem sozinhos.

4 Em "The Korubo's future is secure **as long as** they are left in peace", a expressão *as long as* indica:

a ( ) tempo
b ( ) distância
c ( ) impedimento
d ( ) negação
e ( ) condição

Reading 6

RAFAEL GENTILE

Weight-Loss Surgery Not a Surefire Bet for Superobese

Posted by **Catherine Guthrie**

Weight-loss surgery is often heralded as a relatively risk-free procedure, especially compared to the health problems that can go hand-in-hand with obesity. But, for the heaviest among us – the so-called superobese – the decision to go under the knife is not one to be taken lightly. According to a study published in this month's *Archives of Surgery*, the superobese, especially those with underlying ills, like diabetes, are far more likely to die in the months and years following surgery than those who start out weighing less. (A body-mass index greater than 50 is considered superobese.) Whereas the average 1-year mortality rate for patients undergoing bariatric surgery is estimated to be less than 1 percent per year, the superobese patients who took part in this study had a 5.2 percent risk of mortality, dying within the first year – a five-fold increase. To explain the gap, the authors point out that the more sizable the patient, the more technically difficult the surgery and the greater the risk of complications. Even so, the researchers stopped short of denouncing weight-loss surgery for the biggest of the big. Instead, they note that the superobese "have a high risk of death without surgical treatment" because of their size. In the end, the investigators encourage superobese patients to weigh the potential pros and cons with their doctors before signing up for surgery.

Extracted from <http://wellness.blogs.time.com/2009/10/19/weight-loss-surgery-not-a-surefire-bet-for-superobese-patients>. Accessed on January 27, 2010.

average: média
mortality rate: taxa de mortalidade
pros and cons: prós e contras
sizable: consideravelmente grande
so-called: assim chamados
stopped short: não chegaram a
underlying ills: doenças "silenciosas", que ficam "escondidas" e não provocam sintomas iniciais
weigh: pesar, ponderar
whereas: enquanto

1 **The main idea of a text is the writer's message about the topic. Read the text again and check the alternative that presents the main ideas of the text.**

a ( ) Superobese patients are more likely to die because of surgery complications than other patients.
Superobese patients' risk of mortality is five times greater than anybody else's.

b ( ) One should take undergoing surgery very seriously.
Superobese people undergoing surgery die much sooner than the others.

c ( ) Bariatric surgery is very risky, so doctors advise their patients to consider all possibilities before considering undergoing it.
Doctors should discourage their superobese patients from being operated on.

d ( ) Bariatric surgery may be risky, but sometimes it is the best alternative.
One should always consult his or her doctor before going into surgery.

2 **Assinale V (verdadeiro) ou F (falso) para cada uma das sentenças abaixo.**

		V	F
a	A pessoa cuja massa corporal é inferior a cinquenta é considerada obesa mórbida.		
b	Deve-se pensar muito antes de tomar a decisão de submeter-se a uma cirurgia bariátrica.		
c	Embora haja vários riscos envolvidos em uma cirurgia bariátrica, as doenças causadas pela obesidade podem ser ainda mais prejudiciais.		
d	O diabetes é uma doença muito séria, mas seu diagnóstico nem sempre é fácil, uma vez que se trata de uma doença silenciosa a qual, a princípio, não provoca sintomas sensíveis ao doente, que, portanto, não percebe que há algo de errado.		
e	Os pesquisadores passaram a denunciar médicos que fazem cirurgia bariátrica em pacientes considerados obesos mórbidos.		

3 **Considere as afirmações e assinale a alternativa correta:**

A Em "[...] the decision to go under the knife is not one to be taken lightly.", *one* refere-se a "decisão".

B Em "[...] are far more likely to die in the months and years following surgery than those who start out weighing less.", *those* refere-se às "pessoas que se submetem à cirurgia para redução de peso mas que não são consideradas obesas mórbidas".

C A expressão *the biggest of the big* em "Even so, the researchers stopped short of denouncing weight-loss surgery for the biggest of the big." substitui a palavra *superobese*.

a ( ) Apenas a afirmação A está correta.

b ( ) Apenas as afirmações A e C estão corretas.

c ( ) Apenas a afirmação C está correta.

d ( ) Apenas as afirmações A e B estão corretas.

e ( ) As afirmações A, B e C estão corretas.

Reading 7

Wastewater Treatment

PHOTO: J. L. BULCAO / PULSAR IMAGENS; ART: RAFAEL GENTILE

[...]

Raw sewage includes waste from sinks, toilets, and industrial processes. Treatment of the sewage is required before it can be safely buried, used, or released back into local water systems. In a treatment plant, the waste is passed through a series of screens, chambers, and chemical processes to reduce its bulk and toxicity. The three general phases of treatment are primary, secondary, and tertiary. During primary treatment, a large percentage of the suspended solids and inorganic material is removed from the sewage. The focus of secondary treatment is reducing organic material by accelerating natural biological processes. Tertiary treatment is necessary when the water will be reused; 99 percent of solids are removed and various chemical processes are used to ensure the water is as free from impurity as possible. [...]

Extracted from <http://www.umich.edu/-gS265/society/waterpollution.htm>. Accessed on March 20, 2010.

What are the dangers of water pollution?

Learn about the possible dangers to your health, the environment, and the economy.

Virtually all types of water pollution are harmful to the health of humans and animals. Water pollution may not damage our health immediately but can be harmful after long-term exposure. Different forms of pollutants affect the health of animals in different ways:

- Heavy metals from industrial processes can accumulate in nearby lakes and rivers. These are toxic to marine life such as fish and shellfish, and subsequently to the humans who eat these animals. Heavy metals can slow development; result in birth defects and some are carcinogenic.
- Industrial waste often contains many toxic compounds that damage the health of aquatic animals and those who eat these animals. Some of the toxins in industrial waste may only have a mild effect, whereas others can be fatal. They can cause immune suppression, reproductive failure, or acute poisoning.
- Microbial pollutants from sewage often result in infectious diseases that infect aquatic life and terrestrial life through drinking water. Microbial water pollution is a major problem in the developing world, with diseases such as cholera and typhoid fever being the primary cause of infant mortality.
- Organic matter and nutrients cause an increase in aerobic algae and deplete oxygen from the water column. This causes the suffocation of fish and other aquatic organisms.
- Sulfate particles from acid rain can cause harm the health of marine life in the rivers and lakes it contaminates, and can result in mortality.
- Suspended particles in freshwater reduce the quality of drinking water for humans and the aquatic environment for marine life. Suspended particles can often reduce the amount of sunlight penetrating the water, disrupting the growth of photosynthetic plants and micro-organisms.

Extracted from <http://www.water-pollution.org.uk/health.html>. Accessed on March 20, 2010.

bulk: grande quantidade, grande volume
buried: enterrado
carcinogenic: que favorece o desenvolvimento de um carcinoma
depletes: esgota
harmful: prejudicial
mild: leve, suave
released: lançado
sewage: esgoto

1 **Qual das alternativas abaixo associa corretamente as fases do tratamento de esgoto?**

a ( ) Primária: filtração; secundária: filtração e reações químicas; terciária: filtração.

b ( ) Primária: reações químicas; secundária: filtração e reações químicas; terciária: reações químicas.

c ( ) Primária: filtração; secundária: aceleração de processos biológicos; terciária: filtração e processos químicos.

d ( ) Primária: reações químicas; secundária: filtração; terciária: filtração e reações químicas.

2 **Assinale a alternativa correta.**

a ( ) Apenas os animais marinhos, como peixes e mariscos, são afetados pelo esgoto na água.

b ( ) Os animais terrestres são afetados pelo esgoto somente por meio do consumo de animais marinhos.

c ( ) As plantas não são prejudicadas pela sujeira depositada na água.

d ( ) A princípio, todo tipo de poluição nas águas é danoso para os seres humanos e animais.

3 **Assinale a alternativa que apresenta a soma das alternativas corretas.**

1 A única fonte de poluição aquática é o depósito de esgoto no mar.

2 As partículas de sujeira são prejudiciais a seres que fazem fotossíntese.

4 O consumo de água poluída por metais pesados pode causar defeitos ao feto.

8 O tratamento de esgoto não leva em conta a reutilização da água.

16 Algumas toxinas encontradas no lixo industrial despejado na água podem matar seres humanos.

a ( ) 17 **b** ( ) 22 **c** ( ) 7 **d** ( ) 12 **e** ( ) 15

4 **Qual das alternativas mostra a soma das medidas que não seriam apropriadas para reduzir os efeitos da poluição da água?**

1 Promover uma campanha de vacinação contra cólera e febre tifoide.

2 Dar um destino adequado aos resíduos industriais.

4 Remoção completa da matéria orgânica nos rios e lagos.

8 Aumentar a quantidade de sulfato na água.

16 Tratamento trifásico do esgoto.

a ( ) 29 **b** ( ) 13 **c** ( ) 20 **d** ( ) 24 **e** ( ) 7

5 **Em seu caderno, com base no texto, explique resumidamente o efeito da poluição da água nos animais.**

Reading 8

ancient: muito antigo
fail: falhar
lost your mind: enlouqueceu

1 **Releia a frase do quarto quadrinho e três maneiras de reescrevê-la:**

Original: *"Whatever, who cares?"*

1 Who cares, whatever?

2 Whatever, I don't care.

3 It doesn't matter. Who cares?

O sentido da frase original só <u>não</u> se altera em:

a ( ) 1 e 2 **c** ( ) 1 e 3 **e** ( ) 2 e 3

b ( ) 1 apenas **d** ( ) 2 apenas

2 **Escolha a alternativa que melhor explica o que Sally quis dizer em sua redação (quadrinhos de 3 a 8).**

a ( ) Quando você está em uma situação difícil, o melhor a fazer é pedir ajuda à sua mãe.

b ( ) Mães ajudam os filhos a formular novas filosofias.

c ( ) O grito pela mãe é o mais antigo e desesperado.

d ( ) Quando as filosofias provam-se erradas, as pessoas pedem ajuda às mães.

e ( ) Quando Sally explica aos colegas sua filosofia, eles começam a encará-la como se ela tivesse enlouquecido.

3 **Assinale a alternativa que contém a soma das frases corretas.**

1 No terceiro quadrinho, *it* retoma a palavra *where*.

2 Apenas uma das perguntas que Sally faz no quarto quadrinho é retórica.

4 Sally põe em dúvida sua antiga filosofia, mas não formula uma nova.

8 Não é possível identificar com quem a menina está falando no segundo quadrinho.

16 O sujeito de *asks*, no terceiro quadrinho, é *today*.

a ( ) 3 **c** ( ) 4 **e** ( ) 12

b ( ) 20 **d** ( ) 30

4 **Qual das alternativas contém a soma das frases incorretas?**

1 Pode-se concluir que Sally acha que tudo acabará em uma nova filosofia.

2 "Ma'am", no segundo quadrinho, é um vocativo.

4 Sally afirma que o mais antigo ato dos desesperados é chamar a mãe.

8 Sally afirma que a mãe é sempre quem socorre os desesperados.

16 A garota pergunta aos colegas o que acontece quando uma filosofia não dá certo.

a ( ) 13 **c** ( ) 16 **e** ( ) 24

b ( ) 18 **d** ( ) 14

Appendices

UNIT 1 – LINKING WORDS

Giving Examples

for example	*There are many types of cheese,* ***for example****, mozzarella and cream cheese.*
for instance	*I can play some musical instruments,* ***for instance****, the guitar and the drums.*
namely	*He likes a completely different sport,* ***namely*** *kitesurfing.*

Adding Information

also	*He* ***also*** *writes books.*
and	*My favorite kinds of movies are dramas* ***and*** *comedies.*
apart from	***Apart from*** *David, nobody got hurt.*
as well as	***As well as*** *strong, my boyfriend is really courageous.*
besides	***Besides*** *Joan, many more of your friends will be there.*
furthermore	*People are becoming more responsive to the campaigns.* ***Furthermore****, pollution has been reduced.*
in addition	*They study Physical Education.* ***In addition****, they learn some medicine.*
in addition to	***In addition to*** *strengthening your heart, exercise may strengthen your immunity system.*
moreover	*The apartment was empty.* ***Moreover****, it was dusty.*
too	*The kids love singing,* ***too****.*

Summarizing

in a nutshell	*It was a very long meeting but,* ***in a nutshell****, our project was approved.*
in brief	*I didn't like anything served at the party.* ***In brief****, the food was terrible.*
in conclusion	***In conclusion****, the best way to lose weight is to start a healthy diet.*
in short	*The activity can be a puzzle, a guessing game, or a song –* ***in short****, anything creative.*

in summary	***In summary***, *this book is a great introduction to philosophy.*
to conclude	***To conclude***, *besides being cheaper, going to work by bicycle is also a good way to exercise.*
to summarize	***To summarize***, *he found a very clever solution to the problem.*

Sequencing Ideas

the former… the latter	*He has two daughters: Deborah and Lucy.* ***The former*** *is a dentist,* ***the latter*** *is a very successful lawyer.*
firstly, secondly, finally	***Firstly***, *we have to think about a theme.* ***Secondly***, *we need to come up with ideas for the project. Then,* ***finally***, *we will put everything into practice.*
lastly	***Lastly***, *she put on her coat and left.*
the first point is	***The first point*** *to consider* ***is*** *that the budget is too low.*
the following	***The following*** *step is to test the product.*

Giving a Reason

as	***As*** *he was feeling very sleepy, he went to bed early.*
because	*I'm going to do it* ***because*** *I think it's a good idea.*
because of	*We are running late at the office* ***because of*** *Peter's delay.*
due to / due to the fact that	*She can't speak much* ***due to*** *a sore throat.*
owing to / owing to the fact that	*Denise is exhausted* ***owing to the fact that*** *she hasn't taken vacations in three years.*
since	***Since*** *Mom is not making dinner, I'll have to order some food.*

Giving a Result

as a result	*Martha was promoted* ***as a result*** *of her dedication and good results.*
consequently	*Lynn was fed up with Jim's persistent calls.* ***Consequently***, *she broke up with him.*
so	*It was getting late,* ***so*** *I decided to go back home.*
therefore	*Everyone is wearing heavy coats.* ***Therefore***, *it must be really cold outside.*
this means that	*I didn't get my paycheck.* ***This means that*** *I won't be able to travel this weekend.*

Contrasting Ideas

although / even though	***Although*** *her flight was delayed, Sarah was able to arrive in time for the meeting.*
but	*I could eat this bowl of ice cream,* ***but*** *I'm on a diet.*
despite / despite the fact that	***Despite*** *being a handsome and successful man, Carlo had a hard time finding a girlfriend.*
however	*I would love to buy this car.* ***However****, I don't think I can afford it.*
in spite of / in spite of the fact that	***In spite of*** *her financial problems, Jane didn't accept the job offer.*
in theory... in practice...	***In theory*** *this seems to be a very easy task, but* ***in practice*** *it's not a piece of cake.*
nevertheless	*It was a small mistake, but it was fatal* ***nevertheless****.*
nonetheless	*Sheila was serious, but* ***nonetheless*** *very friendly.*
unlike	***Unlike*** *every other teenager I know, my cousin is not fond of night clubs.*
whereas	*I like going to the beach,* ***whereas*** *my boyfriend prefers going to the movies.*
while	*The movie I rented is fabulous,* ***while*** *that other one is boring.*

UNIT 2 – IDIOMS

a piece of cake: algo muito fácil	*This job is* ***a piece of cake****. I don't need another week to finish it.*
be fed up with: sem paciência, cansado	*I'****m*** *so* ***fed up with*** *Daniel's rudeness!*
be head over heels: estar completamente apaixonado	*Do you believe they met at a bookstore and* ***are now head over heels****?*
be on cloud nine: ficar muito feliz, nas nuvens	*Since she didn't expect to get a promotion (and got it), she'****s on cloud nine*** *now.*
break a leg: boa sorte	*I know you have a test this afternoon.* ***Break a leg****!*
couch potato: alguém que passa muito tempo em frente à TV	*Don't be such a* ***couch potato****, let's do some exercise!*
feel blue: sentir-se triste, deprimido	*I'm* ***feeling blue*** *because I haven't seen my family for quite a long time.*
get cold feet: desistir por falta de coragem	*I was going to ask her out, but I* ***got cold feet****.*
get on one's nerves: irritar alguém	*That girl keeps calling you every 5 minutes. She's* ***getting on my nerves****.*

have the guts: ter coragem para fazer algo	*Do you think he'll **have the guts** to send her that report?*
in the heat of the moment: no calor do momento	*Don't be mad at him, he just said that **in the heat of the moment**.*
jump to conclusions: tirar conclusões precipitadas	*Don't **jump to conclusions**! Just because she hasn't called yet doesn't mean she doesn't miss you.*
keep one's fingers crossed: torcer para o melhor acontecer	*Do you have a job interview tomorrow? I'll **keep my fingers crossed**.*
make up one's mind: tomar uma decisão	*There are so many delicious deserts I just can't **make up my mind**!*

UNIT 3 – FALSE COGNATES

actually (adv) realmente; na verdade	**atualmente** nowadays; today
amass (v) acumular; juntar	**amassar** crush
application (n) registro; uso	**aplicação** investment
appointment (n) hora marcada; compromisso	**apontamento** note
appreciation (n) gratidão; reconhecimento	**apreciação** judgement
argument (n) discussão	**argumento** reasoning; point
assist (v) ajudar, dar apoio	**assistir** attend; watch
assume (v) presumir; aceitar como verdadeiro	**assumir** take over
attend (v) assistir; participar de	**atender** help; answer; see; examine
balcony (n) sacada	**balcão** counter
carton (n) caixa de papelão	**cartão** card
casualty (n) baixas (mortes)	**casualidade** chance
cigar (n) charuto	**cigarro** cigarette
collar (n) gola, colarinho; coleira	**colar** necklace
college (n) faculdade; ensino superior	**colégio** high school
commodity (n) artigo, mercadoria	**comodidade** comfort
comprehensive (adj) abrangente; amplo, extenso	**compreensivo** understandable
compromise (v) entrar em acordo; conceder	**compromisso** appointment
contest (n) competição; concurso	**contexto** context

costume (n) fantasia (roupa)	**costume** custom; habit
data (n) dados (números, informações)	**data** date
deception (n) fraude, logro	**decepção** disappointment
design (v, n) criar; projetar; projeto	**designar** appoint
editor (n) redator	**editor** publisher
educated (adj) instruído; estudado	**educado** well-mannered, polite
enroll (v) inscrever-se; alistar-se; registrar-se	**enrolar** roll; wind; curl
eventually (adv) finalmente, no final	**eventualmente** occasionally
exciting (adj) empolgante	**excitante** thrilling
exit (n, v) saída; sair	**êxito** success
expert (n) especialista, perito	**esperto** smart, clever
exquisite (adj) belo; refinado	**esquisito** strange, odd
fabric (n) tecido	**fábrica** plant, factory
gratuity (n) gratificação, gorjeta	**grátis** free, free of charge
grip (v) agarrar firme	**gripe** cold, flu, influenza
hazard (n, v) risco; arriscar	**azar** bad luck
idiom (n) expressão idiomática	**idioma** language
ingenuity (n) engenhosidade	**ingenuidade** naiveté/naivety
injury (n) ferimento	**injúria** insult; offense
inscription (n) gravação (sobre pedra, metal)	**inscrição** application
intend (v) pretender, ter a intenção	**entender** understand
journal (n) periódico, revista especializada	**jornal** newspaper
large (adj) grande; espaçoso	**largo** wide
lecture (n) palestra	**leitura** reading
legend (n) lenda	**legenda** subtitle
library (n) biblioteca	**livraria** bookshop; bookstore
lunch (n) almoço	**lanche** snack
magazine (n) revista	**magazine** department store
mayor (n) prefeito	**maior** bigger
moisture (n) umidade	**mistura** mix; mixture; blend

notice (n, v) aviso; notar	**notícia** news
novel (n) romance	**novela** soap opera
office (n) escritório	**ofício** profession
parents (n) pais	**parentes** relatives
pasta (n) massa (macarrão)	**pasta** briefcase; folder; paste
policy (n) política	**polícia** police
porter (n) carregador	**porteiro** door keeper
prejudice (n) preconceito	**prejuízo** damage; loss
preservative (n) conservante	**preservativo** condom
pretend (v) fingir	**pretender** intend, plan
procure (v) conseguir, adquirir	**procurar** look for, search for
pull (v) puxar	**pular** jump
push (v) empurrar	**puxar** pull
range (n, v) cadeia (montanhas); variar; cobrir	**ranger** creak; grind
realize (v) notar, perceber	**realizar** accomplish; do
recipient (n) recebedor; agraciado	**recipiente** container
record (v, n) gravar; gravação; registro	**recordar** remember; recall
requirement (n) requisito	**requerimento** request, petition
resume (n) retomar; reiniciar	**resumir** summarize
retired (adj) aposentado	**retirado** removed; secluded
senior (n) idoso	**senhor** gentleman; sir
stranger (n) desconhecido	**estrangeiro** foreigner

Extraído de Hollaender, Arnon & Sanders, Sidney. *Landmark Dictionary para Estudantes Brasileiros de Inglês*. São Paulo: Moderna, 2008, p. 552 – 553.

UNIT 4 – PREPOSITIONS

about	*What is Professor Geller's lecture* ***about****?* *The plane is going to land in* ***about*** *ten minutes.*
after	*Do you believe in life* ***after*** *death?*
against	*He has already played tennis* ***against*** *that famous Russian player.*

at	*Liz and her friend sat down* ***at*** *the table.* *Meet me* ***at*** *8 p.m.*
before	*Come* ***before*** *him. Otherwise you'll meet him.*
besides	*People choose jobs for other reasons* ***besides*** *money.*
beyond	*I can't teach you anything* ***beyond*** *what you already know.*
by	*James walked* ***by*** *and didn't notice me.*
for	*Someone left a message* ***for*** *Vicky.* *Mrs. Stuart hasn't seen her oldest son* ***for*** *years.*
from	*All the information has been extracted* ***from*** *a website.* *David is* ***from*** *New Mexico.*
in	*I've heard that their marriage is* ***in*** *trouble.* *He took us for a drive* ***in*** *his new car last night.* *The actress was dressed* ***in*** *a blue linen suit.* *The teacher's birthday is* ***in*** *August.*
instead of	*Could I have tuna* ***instead of*** *ham?*
of	*Two* ***of*** *the guests are vegetarian.*
on	*The little girl was sitting* ***on*** *her father's shoulders.* *I was born* ***on*** *July 1.*
outside	*The* ***outside*** *of the house was painted white and blue.*
through	*She smiled at him as he walked* ***through*** *the door.*
to	*I was going* ***to*** *the kitchen when they shut off the lights.*
underneath	*She was wearing a jacket with a T-shirt* ***underneath****.*
up	*We walked slowly* ***up*** *the hill.*
with	*Put this bag* ***with*** *the others.*
without	*After the storm we were* ***without*** *electricity for hours.*

UNIT 5 – SIMILAR WORDS

beside *There is a new restaurant* ***beside*** *my house.*	**besides** ***Besides*** *English, she speaks Spanish and Italian.*
dead *His plan to travel around the world has been* ***dead*** *for years.*	**died** *Ayrton Senna* ***died*** *in 1994.*

economic *My family has had **economic** problems. We haven't bought our house yet.*	**economical** *My mother is an **economical** housewife.*
last *He told me it was my **last** chance to solve the problem.*	**latest** *Have you watched George Clooney's **latest** film?*
lose *My husband keeps **losing** his glasses.*	**loose** *My son's pants are too **loose**.*
police *The **police** arrived a few minutes after the crime.*	**policy** *The politician kept changing his **policy**.*
price *What's the **price** of that black T-shirt?*	**prize** *Nelson Mandela received the Nobel Peace **Prize** in 1993.*
sensible *My daughter wants to buy an expensive car. She has to be **sensible** because she doesn't have much money.*	**sensitive** *Don't shout at him. He's very **sensitive**.*
sometime *Let's have lunch **sometime** next weekend.*	**sometimes** *My friends and I **sometimes** travel to the beach on weekends.*

UNIT 6 – PREPOSITIONS AFTER PARTICULAR WORDS AND EXPRESSIONS

ability at	*My son shows great **ability at** soccer.*
afraid of	*Are you **afraid of** snakes?*
angry about	*Why is he so **angry about** traveling to the beach next weekend?*
angry at	*I'm **angry at** my best friend for not telling me the truth.*
bad at	*I'm really **bad at** sports.*
different from	*You are very **different from** your sister.*
difficulty with	*I'm having **difficulty with** my grammar exercises.*
disappointed with	*My grandmother never said she was **disappointed with** me.*
discussion about	*The doctors had a long **discussion about** adolescence.*
dress in	*Who's the guy **dressed in** black?*
example of	*My father is an **example of** loyalty.*

good at	*Is she **good at** drawing?*
impressed with / by	*My boss is very **impressed with / by** my work.*
interest / interested in	*When did her **interest in** Biology begin?* *Many people are **interested in** learning more about biodiversity.*
kind to	*My parents-in-law have always been very **kind to** me.*
reason for	*Nobody knows the **reason for** the murder.*
shocked by / at	*The neighborhood was **shocked at / by** the news of Jane's accident.*
sorry about	*The doctor was **sorry about** her wrong diagnosis.*
sorry for	*I feel **sorry for** his son.*
sorry for / about	*I'm **sorry for / about** loosing your necklace.*
surprised at / by	*Everybody was **surprised at / by** the amazing party last weekend.*
wrong with	*What's **wrong with** you today?*

UNIT 7 – GERUND AND INFINITIVE – DIFFERENCES IN MEANING

	Gerund	Infinitive
begin / start	*She **began playing** the piano when she was eight.* *She **started talking** about politics and everybody left the room.*	*She **began to play** the piano when she was eight.* *She **started to talk** about politics and everybody left the room.*
	There is no important difference between using the gerund or infinitive forms after these verbs.	
forget / remember	*He'll never **forget spending** those days at his cousin's house.* *I **remember switching off** the lights when I went on vacation.*	*Don't **forget to take** some money with you.* ***Remember to switch off** the lights when you go on vacation.*
	These structures look back at the past.	These structures look forward in time.
go on	***Go on reading** the text.*	***Go on to read** the text.*
	= continue	*= a change in activity*
regret	*I **regret leaving** the party early.*	*I **regret to say** I cannot help you with this.*
	This structure talks about something one is sorry one did.	*Regret + infinitive* is used mostly to announce of bad news.

stop	***Stop reading*** *the text.*	***Stop to read*** *the text.*
	= stop the activity	*= stop a past activity to start the activity specified*
try	*Why don't you* ***try running*** *in the morning?*	*I* ***tried to run*** *in the morning, but I had a hard time getting up early.*
	This structure talks about experimenting something new.	This structure talks about making an effort to do something difficult.

UNIT 8 – PREPOSITIONS BEFORE PARTICULAR WORDS AND EXPRESSIONS

This is a list of a few expressions which often cause problems.

in pen, pencil, ink, etc.	*Please, fill out the job application* ***in blue pencil.***
in the rain, snow, etc.	*The kids are playing hide-and-seek* ***in the snow****.* *Don't talk to your sister* ***in that rude voice****.*
in a suit, raincoat, hat, high-heeled shoes, etc.	*Who is that lady* ***in the red high-heeled shoes****?*
at the end (at the point something stops)	*Doctor Fernandez was wrong about the patient's problem* ***at the end****.*
in the end (finally, after a long time)	***In the end****, Mary Ann said yes to Dave's wedding proposal.*
in time (with enough time to spare, not late)	*Last week I missed a job interview because I was stuck in a traffic jam and couldn't arrive* ***in time****.*
on time (at exactly the right time)	*I arrived at the airport* ***on time*** *and said goodbye to my friend Ellie.*
on the radio, on TV	*Tonight we are going to watch a nice comedy* ***on TV****.*

Grammar Review

SIMPLE PRESENT

FORMAÇÃO: VERBO NO INFINITIVO SEM A PARTÍCULA **TO**

Forma afirmativa	I **resolve** to cut back on ice cream.
	He **plays** soccer once a week.
Acrescenta-se **s** à maioria dos verbos para as terceiras pessoas do singular (he, she, it).	

Forma negativa	They **don't work** on weekends.
	She **doesn't have** a bike.
Usam-se **don't** e **doesn't**. Nas terceiras pessoas do singular, os verbos voltam à sua forma de infinitivo.	

Forma interrogativa	**A: Do** you **like** vegetables? **B:** Yes, I do. / No, I don't.
	A: Does he **live** downtown? **B:** Yes, he does. / No, he doesn't.
Usam-se **do** e **does**. Nas terceiras pessoas do singular, os verbos voltam à sua forma de infinitivo.	

FORMAÇÃO DE VERBOS NA TERCEIRA PESSOA DO SINGULAR: CASOS ESPECIAIS

Em verbos que terminam em **ch**, **sh**, **ss**, **x**, **o** ou **z**, acrescenta-se **es**. watch – watch**es** pass – pass**es**
Em verbos que terminam em **y** precedido de consoante, elimina-se o **y** e acrescenta-se **ies**. stud**y** – stud**ies**

USO

O **Simple Present** é utilizado para:	
• Expressar ações que acontecem no dia a dia.	Grandpa goes for a walk in the park every morning. My family gets together for dinner at about 7:00 p.m.
As ações habituais são geralmente expressas com advérbios de frequência, como **always**, **usually**, **frequently**, **often**, **sometimes**, **hardly ever**, **never**, e com expressões como **every day**, **twice a week**, **at 10 o'clock**, etc.	

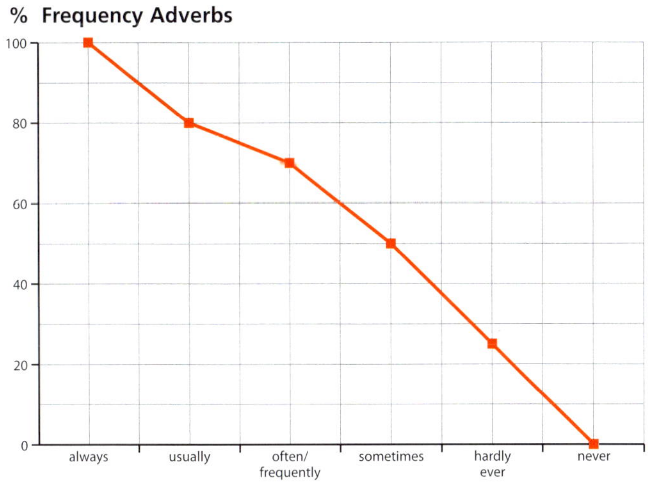 ALESSANDRO PASSOS DA COSTA	My classmates and I **usually** arrive early at school. We **never** go out in the evening. Diana's daughter chats online **three times a week**.
• Fazer referência a fatos permanentes.	Uncle Peter lives in California.
• Falar sobre ações que acontecerão no futuro, com horários ou períodos agendados no presente.	Preacher's kids arrive from the U.S. tomorrow morning.
• Registrar verdades universais e localizações geográficas.	Water boils at 100 degrees centigrade. Brazil lies in South America.

PRESENT CONTINUOUS

FORMAÇÃO: VERBO TO BE NO PRESENTE + VERBO PRINCIPAL + **ING**

Forma afirmativa	The increase in the emission of greenhouse effect gases **is forming** a thick layer of these gases around the Earth.
Acrescenta-se **ing** ao final da maioria dos verbos.	

Forma negativa	She **isn't working** today. She's off.

Forma interrogativa	**A: Are** you **watching** the news? **B:** Yes, I am. / No, I'm not.

FORMAÇÃO DO VERBO PRINCIPAL: CASOS ESPECIAIS	
Nos verbos que terminam em **consoante + e**, elimina-se o **e** e acrescenta-se **ing**.	liv**e** – liv**ing** writ**e** – writ**ing**
Nos verbos que terminam em **consoante + vogal + consoante** e que têm a última sílaba tônica, dobra-se a última consoante e acrescenta-se **ing**.	**put** – pu**tting** be**gin** – beg**inning**

USO

O **Present Continuous** é utilizado para:	
• Descrever ações que acontecem no momento da fala. Geralmente acompanham advérbios de tempo como **now**, **at the moment**, etc.	The teacher is talking about global warming **now**. Listen! They are playing the guitar.
• Expressar ações que estão ocorrendo por um determinado período ou nos dias atuais.	This semester the students are reading up on the increase in the planet's temperature. Most people around the world are changing some of their habits to save our planet.
• Falar sobre ações que foram agendadas, planejadas ou confirmadas anteriormente.	My classmates and I are visiting the planetarium on Monday. Mr. Johnson is coming to the office at noon.
• Alguns verbos em inglês não são utilizados com **ing**, tais como *love, hate, like, prefer, remember, forget, understand, know, need,* etc.	We know that we can all help reduce the threat of global warming. Do you understand how temperature rise occurs?

FUTURE WITH *GOING TO*

FORMAÇÃO: VERBO TO BE NO PRESENTE + **GOING TO** + VERBO PRINCIPAL

Forma afirmativa	The students **are going to read** about internet traffic.
Forma negativa	Melissa **isn't going to swim** today. She's tired.
Forma interrogativa	**A: Are** you **going to write** that text in Mandarin? **B:** Yes, I am. / No, I'm not.

USO

O futuro com **going to** é utilizado para:	
• Falar sobre eventos ou situações que acontecerão no futuro com base em evidências do presente.	The present statistics show that the number of internet users in Brazil is going to grow more and more.
• Expressar intenções ou planos futuros e previsões.	Dad is going to buy a new car in December. Those students are going to use the internet in class next year.
• Geralmente vem acompanhado de advérbios de tempo como **tomorrow**, **next**, etc.	

IMPERATIVES

FORMAÇÃO: VERBO NO INFINITIVO SEM A PARTÍCULA **TO**

Forma afirmativa	**Open** that door, please. It's hot in here.
Forma negativa	**Don't call** Jimmy now. He's studying.

USO

O **imperative** é utilizado para:	
• Expressar uma ordem.	Help your mom in the kitchen, Audrey. She's late with lunch.
• Fazer pedidos.	Ask David to download the video about e-commerce spending.
• Dar instruções.	Press the button before you use the equipment.

PERSONAL PRONOUNS

Subject	Object
I	me
you	you
he	him
she	her
it	it
we	us
you	you
they	them

USO

Os **subject pronouns** são usados como sujeito em uma oração. Os **object pronouns** são usados como objeto direto ou indireto.	**She** likes Aunt Sophie. Aunt Sophie likes **her** too.

SIMPLE PAST

Forma afirmativa	Tarsila do Amaral **initiated** her Pau-Brasil phase.
Forma negativa	Mike **didn't go** to work by car this morning.
Usa-se **didn't** e o verbo volta à sua forma de infinitivo.	

Forma interrogativa	**A: Did** the students **organize** the art exhibition? **B:** Yes, they did. / No, they didn't.
Usa-se **did** e o verbo volta à sua forma de infinitivo.	

FORMAÇÃO DE VERBOS REGULARES

Regra geral: verbo no infinitivo sem a partícula **to** + **ed**.	work – work**ed**
Casos especiais:	
• Em verbos que terminam em **e**, acrescenta-se **d**.	lik**e** – like**d** decid**e** – decide**d**
• Em verbos que terminam em **y** precedido de **consoante**, elimina-se o **y** e acrescenta-se **ied**.	stud**y** – stud**ied** marr**y** – marr**ied**
• Em verbos que terminam em **consoante** + **vogal** + **consoante**, cuja sílaba tônica é a última, dobra-se a última consoante e acrescenta-se **ed**.	st**op** – sto**pped** per**mit** – permi**tted**

FORMAÇÃO DE VERBOS IRREGULARES

Não há uma regra geral. Recomenda-se a aprendizagem pelo uso constante dos verbos.	be – was, were buy – bought come – came cut – cut
As formas negativa e interrogativa do verbo **to be** não necessitam do uso do auxiliar **did**.	The students **weren't** tired after the sports competition. **Were** you at the club at this time yesterday?

USO

O **Simple Past** é utilizado para:	
• Expressar ações que terminaram em um tempo determinado. Neste caso, advérbios de tempo e expressões adverbiais (**yesterday**, **last week**, **in 2008**, **three days ago**, etc.) são geralmente utilizados.	Tarsila do Amaral returned to São Paulo **in 1922**. My parents bought a very expensive painting **last week**.
• Indicar hábitos no passado.	I went to my grandparents' house on Sundays **when I was little**.

PAST CONTINUOUS

FORMAÇÃO: VERBO TO BE NO PASSADO + VERBO PRINCIPAL + **ING**

Forma afirmativa	I **was** read**ing** an article about urban tribes ten minutes ago.
Forma negativa	It **wasn't** rain**ing** at 10 a.m. The day was wonderful.
Forma interrogativa	**A: Were** the kids play**ing** in the yard before lunch? **B:** Yes, they were. / No, they weren't.

USO

O **Past Continuous** é utilizado para:	
• Expressar ações em progresso em um determinado período no passado.	My neighbors were cleaning the house at 9:00. I was working on my project at this time yesterday.
• Descrever uma ação que estava ocorrendo quando outra aconteceu.	When I saw Jane and her sister, they were talking to a *cumbiero*. My friends and I were jogging when it started to rain.
• Indicar duas ou mais ações que ocorreram ao mesmo tempo no passado.	My brother was chatting while I was sleeping. While Aunt Betsy and Uncle Joseph were cooking, we were setting the table.

POSSESSIVE ADJECTIVES AND PRONOUNS

Possessive adjectives	Possessive pronouns
my	mine
your	yours
his	his
her	hers
its	its
our	ours
your	yours
their	theirs

USO

Os **possessive adjectives** são posicionados antes de substantivos.	This is **my** computer. Look! Swellen is wearing **her** black skirt again.
Os **possessive pronouns** substituem os substantivos aos quais se referem.	I'm eating **my** sandwich now. Are you eating **yours** (your sandwich)?
Os **possessive pronouns** podem ser usados em expressões como: a friend of..., a relative of..., an enemy of..., etc.	A friend of **mine** is coming for holidays.

MODAL VERBS

Os verbos modais (**can**, **could**, **must**, **may**, **might** e **should**) são verbos auxiliares que dão um significado específico para o verbo principal.
Esses verbos: • são utilizados no infinitivo sem **to**; • precedem o verbo principal; • têm a mesma forma para todas as pessoas; • não necessitam de outros verbos auxiliares para as formas negativas e interrogativas.

USO

Can, Could (pode, podia, poderia)	
São utilizados para:	
• Expressar capacidade e habilidade.	Stem cell therapy can repair a damaged tissue. Geoffrey could read when he was four.
Formas negativas: can't / couldn't	
• Expressar capacidade ou habilidade, **can** e **could** podem ser substituídos por **be able to**.	The students can understand what stem cells are used for. ⇓ The students are able to understand what stem cells are used for. Could Patrick swim well when he was young? ⇓ Was Patrick able to swim well when he was young?
Formas negativas: am not / aren't / isn't able to (present) wasn' / weren't (past)	
• Expressar um pedido, solicitar ou conceder permissão e oferecer ajuda.	Could you please send me the article about technology and health? **A:** Can I use your cell phone for a minute? **B:** Yes, you can. / No, you can't. You can open the door now, John. Can I help you with lunch?

Must (deve)	
É utilizado para:	
• Expressar obrigação e dedução.	Candidates must arrive thirty minutes before the exam. Derek must be tired after his soccer practice. After all, he has been playing for three hours.
Na forma negativa, *must not* (*mustn't*) indica proibição.	Students mustn't use their cell phones in class.

Have to pode ser utilizado no lugar de *must* para indicar *obrigação*, sem alteração de sentido.	Those scientists must learn more about stem cell transplants. ⇓ Those scientists have to learn more about stem cell transplants.
Formas negativas: don't/doesn't have to	
• Expressar uma obrigação no passado, usa-se *had to*.	Dr. Phillip had to go to his office last Saturday.
Forma negativa: didn't have to	

May, might (pode, podia, poderia)	
São utilizados para:	
• Expressar possibilidade e dedução. Para expressar possibilidade, **might** é menos usado do que **may**, por ser mais formal.	The body's ability to grow may fail sometimes. Many health problems might be treated by stem cells.
• **May** também pode ser utilizado para fazer um pedido, pedir ou dar permissão e oferecer ajuda num contexto mais formal.	May I talk to you, Mr. Bennett? You may take the day off next Saturday, Ray. Hello, Mrs. Smith. May I help you with the bags?
• Expressar permissão, **may** pode ser substituído por **be allowed to**.	You may ask questions to the chairman now. ⇓ You are allowed to ask questions to the chairman now.
Formas negativas: am not / aren't / isn't allowed to (present) wasn't / weren't allowed to (past)	

Should (deve, deveria)	
• É utilizado para expressar conselho ou recomendação.	You should go to work on foot twice a week. Our students should read articles about organic foods.
Forma negativa: shouldn't	

COUNTABLE AND UNCOUNTABLE NOUNS

Os substantivos podem ser classificados em contáveis (*countable*) ou incontáveis (*uncountable*).	
Os substantivos contáveis recebem a forma do singular ou do plural. No apêndice da unidade 5, na página 162, vimos que há diferentes maneiras de se fazer a forma plural dos substantivos. Se julgar necessário, consulte o apêndice novamente. Os substantivos contáveis podem ser precedidos por:	
• Artigos definidos ou indefinidos	**the** flower **a** floating boat **the** boats **an** orchard
• **Many** (muitos, muitas)	There are **many** floating markets around the city.
• **A few** (alguns, algumas)	We should plant more flowers in our garden. There are only **a few** flowers now.
• **Few** (poucos, poucas)	That poor girl has **few** toys to play with.

Os substantivos incontáveis são apenas usados no singular. Podem ser precedidos por:	
• **Much** (muito, muita)	John doesn't have **much** time to write long reports.
• **A little** (algum, alguma)	The child has **a little** money to buy a candy bar.
• **Little** (pouco, pouca)	There was **little** time for the tourists to see Hindu pilgrims in the Ganges.

Notas

Plenty of, **a lot of** e **lots of** podem substituir **much** e **many**, principalmente em frases afirmativas.	The room needs **plenty of** (much) fresh air. Patrick took **a lot of** (much) money when he traveled last May. Mom bought **lots of** (many) vegetables for the week.
Algumas expressões podem ser utilizadas para indicar a quantidade de substantivos incontáveis.	**a cup of** coffee **a slice of** bread **a glass of** cold tea **a bottle of** water **a jug of** juice **a can of** soda **a piece of** cake **a carton of** milk
Alguns substantivos incontáveis são usados no plural para expressar significados específicos:	"Small wooden boats laden with **fruits** [...]" (frutas diversas) "[...] in the sacred **waters** of the Ganges." (nas águas sagradas do Ganges)

COMPARISON OF ADJECTIVES

Os adjetivos podem ser utilizados em dois graus: *comparative* e *superlative*. No primeiro caso, quando se quer comparar as características que esses adjetivos atribuem aos substantivos; no segundo caso, quando se quer intensificá-las.

Comparative (comparando dois itens)	
O grau comparativo pode ser de:	
• Igualdade (tão... quanto)	These dresses are **as fashionable as** those ones.
• Inferioridade (menos... do que)	Bob's sneakers are **less expensive than** mine.
• Superioridade (mais... do que) Ao final de adjetivos de uma sílaba normalmente acrescentamos **er**. O mesmo acontece com alguns adjetivos de duas sílabas; outros, no entanto, são acompanhados de **more... than**. Já todos os adjetivos com três sílabas ou mais são sempre acompanhados de **more... than**.	The Simpsons **are richer than** the Jacobs. That street behind the park **is narrower than** the one in front of the market. My uncle's car is **more modern than** my aunt's. My young brother's cap is **more sophisticated than** my old brother's.
Superlative (comparando um item aos demais)	
O grau superlativo pode ser de:	
• Inferioridade	She is **the least optimistic** person in the group.
• Superioridade Ao final de adjetivos de uma sílaba, normalmente acrescentamos **est**. O mesmo acontece com alguns adjetivos de duas sílabas; outros, no entanto, são acompanhados de **the most**...	Jason is **the tallest** boy in my class. That was **the simplest** thing the Geography teacher said today. We had **the most delicious** meals in Rome when we were in Europe.

Notas

Em adjetivos terminados em **e**, acrescenta-se somente **r** ou **st**.	lat**e** lat**er** than the lat**est**
Em adjetivos terminados em **consoante** + **vogal** + **consoante**, dobra-se a última consoante antes do acréscimo de **er** ou **est**.	big big**ger** than the big**gest**
Em adjetivos terminados em **y**, elimina-se o **y** e acrescenta-se **ier** ou **iest**.	happ**y** happ**ier** than the happ**iest**
Comparações irregulares:	good – better than – the best bad – worse than – the worst far – farther/further than – the farthest/the furthest

SIMPLE FUTURE

FORMAÇÃO: **WILL** + VERBO NO INFINITIVO SEM A PARTÍCULA **TO**

Forma afirmativa	In coming years, biopiracy **will cause** traditional populations to lose control over their resources.
Forma negativa	Flora and fauna **won't** (**will** + **not**) **disappear** from Brazil in the next few years.
Forma interrogativa	**A: Will** the Amazon rainforest **recover** from deforestation? **B:** Yes, it will. / No, it won't.

USO

O **Simple Future** é utilizado para:	
• Expressar ação ou previsão quanto ao futuro.	We **will** never **forget** about our teacher Ms. Miller.
• Fazer um pedido.	**Will** you please **bring** me your umbrella?
Geralmente vem acompanhado de advérbios ou expressões como **tomorrow**, **next...**, **in...**, **on...**, etc.	

FUTURE CONTINUOUS

FORMAÇÃO: **WILL BE** + VERBO + **ING**

Forma afirmativa	Class 101 **will be going** on a field trip at 7 o'clock tomorrow.
Forma negativa	The Gordons **won't be traveling** abroad on their next vacation.
Forma interrogativa	**Will** you **be working** tomorrow morning?

USO

O **Future Continuous** é utilizado para:	
• Expressar uma ação que estará ocorrendo em um determinado tempo no futuro.	Third-world communities are sure they **will be paying** a high price for biopiracy in the future.

PRESENT PERFECT

FORMAÇÃO: **HAVE/HAS** + PARTICÍPIO PASSADO DO VERBO PRINCIPAL	
Forma afirmativa	Several companies **have responded** to the CBVE survey. Your company **has taken** part in a volunteering project.
Forma negativa	Unfortunately, volunteering **hasn't become** a habit in Brazil. Many industries **haven't motivated** their employees to work on behalf of others.
Forma interrogativa	**A: Have** you **helped** any charitable organizations? **B:** Yes, I have./No, I haven't. **A: Has** she **gained** experience through volunteering? **B:** Yes, she has./No, she hasn't.
Formas abreviadas	**'ve** = have **'s** = has **haven't** = have not **hasn't** = has not

USO

O **Present Perfect** é utilizado para indicar ações que aconteceram em um passado indefinido. Essas ações podem ter terminado ou ainda estar ocorrendo.	I have studied English here for ten years.
Pode ser usado com:	
• Since (desde)	I have known him **since** 1990.
• For (por)	They haven't been married **for** so long.
• Just (recentemente)	I can smell her perfume in the air. She has **just** left.
• Ever (alguma vez, já)	Have you **ever** traveled abroad?
• Never (nunca)	They have **never** tried Japanese food.
• Already (já)	Summer has **already** begun.
• Yet (ainda, já)	I left my CV at the store but they haven't called me for an interview **yet**. Has your mom heard the good news **yet**?
• Lately, recently (ultimamente, recentemente)	We haven't seen her in the neighborhood **recently**. Has she moved away?
• Many times (muitas vezes)	Has the little boy visited his grandma **many times** this month?

PRESENT PERFECT x SIMPLE PAST

O **Simple Past** refere-se a ações totalmente concluídas no tempo passado.	What Mandela **said** about courage **in 1994** is still true.
Já o **Present Perfect** refere-se a ações iniciadas no passado que ainda podem estar em andamento no presente, ou que ocorreram no passado, mas não podemos precisar quando.	Chico Mendes **has taught** the world how important it is to preserve the Amazon.

PRESENT PERFECT CONTINUOUS

FORMAÇÃO: **HAVE/HAS BEEN** + VERBO PRINCIPAL + **ING**

Forma afirmativa	Barack Obama **has been working** as a community activist since his youth.
Forma negativa	Barack Obama **hasn't been working** as a community activist since his youth.
Forma interrogativa	**A: Has** Barack Obama **been working** as a community activist since his youth? **B:** Yes, he has. / No, he hasn't.
Formas abreviadas	**'s** = has **hasn't** = has not **haven't** = have not

USO

O **Present Perfect Continuous** é utilizado para expressar uma ação iniciada no passado e que ainda está em progresso por um período de tempo não específico. É frequentemente usado com *how long* para fazer perguntas e com *for*, *since* e *lately* nas formas afirmativas.	**A:** How long has the politician been leading the country? **B:** He has been leading the country for 5 years.

PAST PERFECT

FORMAÇÃO: **HAD** + PARTICÍPIO PASSADO DO VERBO PRINCIPAL

Forma afirmativa	We **had read** the poem before we wrote the essay.
Forma negativa	We **hadn't read** the poem before we wrote the essay.
Forma interrogativa	**A: Had** you **read** the poem before you wrote the essay? **B:** Yes, we had. / No, we hadn't.
Formas abreviadas	**'d** = had **hadn't** = had not

USO

O **Past Perfect** é utilizado para indicar a ocorrência de uma ação no passado, antes de outra ação também no passado. Usamos o **Simple Past** para indicar a segunda ação ocorrida no passado.	When the ambulance arrived, the poor man had already died. ⇓ (2nd action) ⇓ (1st action) The play hadn't started when I arrived at the theater. ⇓ (1st action) ⇓ (2nd action)
O **Past Perfect** geralmente vem acompanhado de palavras como **when**, **after**, **before**, **already**, **yet**.	

PAST PERFECT CONTINUOUS

FORMAÇÃO: **HAD BEEN** + VERBO PRINCIPAL + **ING**

Forma afirmativa	The singer **had been carrying** his sorrow songs all the way from Africa to Georgia.
Forma negativa	The singer **hadn't been carrying** his sorrow songs all the way from Africa to Georgia.
Forma interrogativa	**A: Had** the singer **been carrying** his sorrow songs all the way from Africa to Georgia? **B:** Yes, he had. / No, he hadn't.

USO

O **Past Perfect Continuous** é utilizado para expressar uma ação que estava acontecendo no passado antes de uma outra ação também no passado. Damos ênfase à ação que ocorreu primeiro entre ações no passado.	The children hadn't been waiting for a long time when their parents picked them up. How long had the players been exercising when the match started? They had been exercising for 15 minutes when the match started.

REFLEXIVE PRONOUNS

myself	yourself	himself	herself	itself
ourselves	yourselves	themselves		

USO

Os **reflexive pronouns** são usados quando o sujeito faz e sofre a ação do verbo; ou seja, sujeito e objeto do verbo são a mesma pessoa. Neste caso, o **reflexive pronoun** é posicionado após o verbo e concorda com o sujeito.	**The wife** couldn't control **herself** and ended up arguing with her husband in public.

Quando queremos dar ênfase ao sujeito ou ao objeto, o **reflexive pronoun** é posicionado logo após o sujeito ou no fim da oração.	**The students themselves** talked to the principal. (ênfase no sujeito) **The students** talked to the principal **themselves**. (ênfase no sujeito) The students talked to **the principal himself**. (ênfase no objeto)
Quando queremos dar a ideia de "sozinho" ou "sem ajuda", o **reflexive pronoun** é precedido de *by*.	Jack was sitting **by himself** in the corner of the café.

Notas

É possível usar o **reflexive pronoun** também após a construção *adjetivo + preposição*.	I'm **proud of myself** for winning the competition.
Alguns verbos, como *wash*, *dress* e *shave*, não têm a sua forma reflexiva em inglês.	Does your father **shave** every day?
Entretanto, a forma reflexiva pode ser utilizada se for necessário deixar claro quem fez a ação.	My son is seven years old so he can **dress himself** now. There are five people in my family. My mom **herself washes** all the family's clothes.

TAG QUESTIONS

FORMAÇÃO: VERBO AUXILIAR/MODAL + PRONOME

Declaração afirmativa – *tag question* negativa	The meeting is on Saturday, **isn't it**?
Declaração negativa – *tag question* afirmativa	You just don't understand, **do you**?

USO

Tag questions são pedidos de confirmação do que foi dito anteriormente em forma de perguntas.	
Casos especiais	I am right, **am I not/aren't I**? Let's go, **shall we**? Don't come back here, **will you**? She may call, **may she not**? There were no mistakes, **were there**? Everybody has a PC, **don't they**?

SOME, ANY, NO

Some e **any** podem ter a função de adjetivos (quando acompanham o substantivo) ou de pronome (quando substituem o substantivo).	**Some** four children die every minute in developing countries from diseases caused by unsafe water. **A:** Do you have **any** money with you? **B:** Yes, I have **some**. / No, I don't have **any**.

USO

Some (algum, alguns, alguma, algumas, um pouco de) Em frases afirmativas ou interrogativas que indiquem ofertas, sugestão ou convite, ou quando se aguarda uma resposta afirmativa.	We need to buy some sodas for the party. Would you like some coffee? Do you mind if I put on some music here?
Any (algum, alguns, algumas, nenhum, nenhuma) Em frases negativas e interrogativas.	I don't know any famous actors. Do you have any questions?

Notas

Any também é utilizado em sentenças afirmativas.	
a) Se o sentido for "qualquer".	Alternative low-cost technologies will be a global standard at any moment.
b) Se estiver precedido de uma condição com **if** (se).	**If** you have any environmental concerns, don't discharge untreated domestic wastewater.
c) Se estiver acompanhando palavras de sentido negativo como **never**, **rarely**, **seldom**, **hardly ever**, **without**, etc.	Some countries **rarely** have any good sanitation conditions.
No / None (nenhum, nenhuma) Em negações, sem haver outra palavra negativa na sentença.	They have **no** solution for the problem. We have **none** either.

O uso de **some, any** e **no** é válido para o emprego de seus compostos.		
somebody / someone	something	somewhere
anybody / anyone	anything	anywhere
nobody / no one	nothing	nowhere

RELATIVE PRONOUNS

Os **relative pronouns** unem uma oração ao seu antecedente, um substantivo. Eles introduzem as orações que indicam a qual pessoa, objeto, animal ou ideia o locutor se refere.	
Who refere-se a pessoas.	The Indians **who** live in Brazil speak a huge number of languages.
Whom refere-se a pessoas. É utilizado quando o pronome relativo for objeto do verbo. Após preposições.	A native Indian leader **whom** I look up to is Raoni. Raoni was the Caiapó tribe chief with **whom** the famous singer Sting worked on behalf of Xingu National Park.
Which refere-se a animais, objetos e ideias.	The Indian tribes **which** are effectively uncontacted live by hunting and gathering in the Amazon.
Whose indica relação de posse. É seguido por um substantivo e nunca pode ser omitido.	The Indian tribes **whose** values were learned from their ancestors believe we should preserve the Earth.
That refere-se a pessoas, objetos e/ou animais. É utilizado após superlativos e palavras como **some**, **any**, **no**, **everything**, **much**, **little**, **only** e **all**. Não é usado entre vírgulas.	The rainforest **that** we consider the biggest reserve in the world is Xingu National Park.
Where é usado como pronome relativo para se referir a lugares.	The environments **where** Brazil's tribal peoples live are tropical forests, grassland, scrub forest, and semi-desert.
When refere-se a dia, mês, etc.	My mom still remembers **when** I started to walk.
What refere-se a objetos, assuntos – algo determinado.	My brother didn't talk about **what** had happened yesterday.

CONDITIONAL SENTENCES (IF CLAUSES)

Conditional sentences são orações que expressam condições. Apresentam diferentes combinações de tempos verbais e vêm relacionadas a orações principais.	
Zero Conditional	
Utilizado para falar sobre uma verdade universal ou para dar uma ordem ou instrução.	If you **heat** water to 100 °C, it **boils**. (heat: Simple Present; boils: Simple Present) If you **need** help, **call** me. (need: Simple Present; call: Imperative)

First Conditional

Utilizado para expressar uma ação possível de acontecer no futuro.	If she **comes** earlier, she **will meet** him. (comes = Simple Present; will meet = Simple Future) If they **don't study**, they **won't have** good grades. (don't study = Simple Present; won't have = Simple Future)

Second Conditional

Utilizado para expressar uma ação que não é real ou não é provável de acontecer.	If I **had** money, I **would lend** you some. (had = Simple Past; would lend = would + verb) We **wouldn't be** lost if we **bought** a map. (wouldn't be = would + verb; bought = Simple Past)

Notas

If pode ser usado no início da frase ou no meio das duas partes da frase. Observe o uso ou não da vírgula.	**If** he pays me, I'll iron his shirts for him. They'll wash the car **if** it doesn't rain.
Na linguagem informal, em frases com **if**, **was** é mais utilizado do que **were**. Na linguagem formal, **were** é mais comum que **was**.	If she **were** my mother, I would forgive her. The teacher would choose me if I **weren't** a bad student.
Unless pode ser usado em lugar de **if... not**.	**If we don't** do something now, global warming will get worse. **Unless** we do something now, global warming will get worse.

Third Conditional

Utilizado para expressar uma ação que não se concretizou no passado e sua provável consequência.	If the students **had taken** some time off, (had taken = Past Perfect) they **would have been** better prepared to (would have been = would have + Past Participle) start another school year.

Nota

Verbos modais (*can*, *may*, *might* e *could*) também podem ser usados nas três frases condicionais.	If I **have** time, I **can/may help** you with the housework. If I **had** R$ 300,00, I **might buy** a new bike. If Joseph **had run fast**, he **could have won** the competition.

DIRECT AND INDIRECT SPEECH (I)

Para relatar o que uma pessoa disse, usamos o discurso direto ou o discurso indireto:	
Direct speech: reproduz exatamente o que foi dito pela pessoa. Aspas são usadas.	The teacher said, "We are going to have a test tomorrow."
Indirect speech: conta o que foi dito, usando nossas palavras. Aspas não são usadas e o uso de *that* é opcional.	The teacher said (that) we / they were going to have a test the next day.

Para usarmos o discurso indireto, fazemos algumas modificações nas frases. Observe:

Direct Speech	Indirect Speech
He said, "I **need** to work late **today**." (Simple Present)	He said (that) he **needed** to work late **that day**. (Simple Past)
He said, "I **met** Sue **yesterday**." (Simple Past)	He said (that) he **had met** Sue **the day before**. (Past Perfect)
She said, "I **will** go shopping **tomorrow**." (will)	She said (that) she **would** go shopping **the next day**. (would)
She said, "I **am studying now**." (Present Continuous)	She said (that) she **was studying then**. (Past Continuous)
They said, "We **were eating** 5 minutes **ago**." (Past Continuous)	They said (that) they **had been eating** 5 minutes **before**. (Past Perfect Continuous)
They said, "We **have finished our** task." (Present Perfect)	They said (that) they **had finished their** task. (Past Perfect)
She said "I **have been studying** English for seven years." (Present Perfect Continuous)	She sais she **had been studying** English for seven years. (Past Perfect Continuous)
Mark said, "We **had gone** there before." (Past Perfect)	Mark said (that) they **had gone** there before. (Past Perfect)

Com *modal verbs*, também temos algumas mudanças:

Direct Speech	Indirect Speech
I said, "I **can** arrange **this** party."	I said (that) I **could** arrange **that** party.
He said, "I **must** have a computer to do **my** job."	He said (that) he **had to** have a computer to do **his** job.
She said, "I **may** open the window."	She said (that) she **might** open the window.

Notas	
Quando o verbo da oração do *direct speech* está no *Simple Present, Future* ou *Present Perfect*, não há mudança obrigatória no tempo verbal da oração no *indirect speech*.	He says, "I **live** in the suburbs." He says (that) he **lives** in the suburbs.

DIRECT AND INDIRECT SPEECH (II)

Podemos reportar as perguntas para o discurso indireto de duas formas.	She said, "Does this restaurant accept credit cards?" She **asked if** that restaurant accepted credit cards. The old man said, "What time is it?" The old man **asked what time** it was.
Em ambos os casos, as perguntas foram transformadas em frases afirmativas. As perguntas iniciadas com auxiliares devem apresentar o uso de **if** (linguagem formal) ou **whether** (linguagem informal). As perguntas iniciadas com pronomes interrogativos devem repetir seu uso.	
Usamos a forma do infinitivo do verbo para relatar ordens ou pedidos expressos pelos verbos **ask**, **tell** e **order**.	Dad said to us, "Come back home before midnight." Dad **asked us to come back** home before midnight. Dad **told us to come back** home before midnight. Dad **ordered us to come back** home before midnight. Dad said to us, "Don't arrive late again." Dad **asked us not to arrive** late again.

FUTURE PERFECT

FORMAÇÃO: **WILL HAVE** + PARTICÍPIO DO VERBO PRINCIPAL

Forma afirmativa	The Jorge Amado Foundation **will have developed** several cultural activities by 2020.
Forma negativa	The story of Gabriela and Nacib Saad in *Gabriela, Clove, and Cinnamon* **won't (will + not) have ceased** to enchant readers by the next decades.
Forma interrogativa	**Will** many people **have read** *Captains of the Sands* by 10 years from now? Yes, they will. / No, they won't.

USO	
O **Future Perfect** é utilizado para expressar uma ação que terá (ou não) acontecido antes de um determinado momento no futuro.	The students **will have finished** the project by the end of the month.

Nota

O **Future Continuous** (will be + verbo + ing) expressa uma ação que estará ocorrendo em um determinado tempo no futuro.	I **will be working** next weekend.

PASSIVE STRUCTURES

FORMAÇÃO: **TO BE** (NO MESMO TEMPO DO VERBO PRINCIPAL) + PARTICÍPIO PASSADO DO VERBO PRINCIPAL

This new virus (2009 H1N1) **was** first **detected** in people in the United States in April 2009.

USO

A **passive structure** é utilizada:	
• Para enfatizar a ocorrência de uma ação e não quem a executou. Assim, só mencionamos o autor da ação (agente da passiva) se for necessário ou importante.	A new road **is being built**. *Mona Lisa* **was painted** by Leonardo da Vinci.
• Em textos técnicos, científicos e reportagens.	A vaccine **has been provided**.

Notas

Em manchetes de jornal/cronologias, a voz passiva geralmente vem sem o verbo *to be*.	This new virus first detected in April 2009. (was first detected)
Quando transformamos uma frase da voz ativa para a voz passiva:	
• O objeto da voz ativa torna-se o sujeito da voz passiva.	
• O verbo *to be* é usado obrigatoriamente no tempo verbal principal da ativa.	
• O verbo principal é usado no *Past Participle*.	

Nota

Quando for mencionado quem fez a ação, usa-se *by* + o agente.	
Quando há dois objetos (um direto e um indireto), a transformação pode ocorrer de duas formas:	Ativa: He didn't send me a note. Passiva 1: I **wasn't sent** a note (by him). Passiva 2: A note **wasn't sent** to me.

INFINITIVE AND GERUND FORMS

INFINITIVE	
FORMAÇÃO: **TO** + VERBO	
USO	
George Daniel has said that his group will not allow able-bodied people **to represent** DPI in the future. He also told us **not to look down on** the disabled. Merle Khoza said disabled people were the best **to articulate** the issued facing them.	
O infinitivo com **to** pode ser usado como sujeito da oração:	To combat discrimination is to understand the issues faced by disabled people.
FORMAÇÃO: VERBO SEM **TO**	
USO	
É usado depois dos verbos modais (*can*, *may*, *should*), dos verbos *make* e *let* e depois de *but* e *except*.	Let me warn you about the dangers of living alone. Honesty makes me feel good. We were so touched by his life story that we did nothing but join the DPI.

GERUND	
FORMAÇÃO: VERBO + **ING** (= substantivo)	
USO	
Como sujeito ou objeto.	Spending all your money before Christmas wasn't a clever idea. Irresponsible Chris didn't stop smoking after she found out she was sick.
Depois de preposições.	Are you interested in improving your fluency?
Depois de alguns verbos/expressões, tais como: *appreciate*, *avoid*, *can't help*, *can't stand*, *consider*, *deny*, *enjoy*, *finish*, *keep*, *mind*, *suggest*, etc.	After listening to his sad tale, I couldn't help crying. Do you mind passing me the salt?
Verbos de percepção (*feel*, *hear*, *listen to*, *look at*, *smell*, *taste*, *touch*, *see*, *watch*) podem ser usados no gerúndio ou no infinitivo sem **to**. São usados no gerúndio quando a ação está/estava em progresso. São usados no infinitivo sem **to** quando a ação foi observada, sentida, do início ao fim.	I saw the couple dancing. (Não vi toda a dança, ela estava em progresso quando a vi.) I saw the couple dance. (Vi toda a dança do casal, do início ao fim.)

Transcripts

LANGUAGE IN ACTION 1. Track 2. page 37

Susan: I work more than anything. When I feel stressed, I eat chocolate, take a long hot shower, drink a lovely cup of tea, and watch TV before I sleep.

Owen: I get stressed when my parents ask me when I'm going to get married. They do that in front of my girlfriend. What do I do then? I take my girlfriend home and then go to the gym to exercise.

David: I really feel stressed when I have to wait in line for a long time or when I need some information urgently and I can't get it. Well, what do I do in these cases? Nothing, in fact.

LANGUAGE IN ACTION 2. Track 3. page 67

Helen: I have been planning to travel around the world for some time, but I can't take any time off. My boss always gives me new projects. I like working outside the home and I do love my job. But I'm exhausted. I have been working hard since my husband got fired from his last job three years ago.

Sara: I'm tired of staying home and looking after my two children. I haven't had a job since I first got pregnant. That was eight years ago. I want to find a job again, but my husband always says I should stay home and take care of our children until they are ten.

Amanda: My husband decided to run his own business right after we got married. The thing is he hasn't been doing well in his business since he started. That was five years ago. It's a non-profit business and my husband hasn't found good professionals to work with him. We have a baby now, but he's never at home with us.

LANGUAGE IN ACTION 3. Track 4. page 97

Mike: You don't look very well. Are you all right, Angela?

Angela: No, I have been feeling terrible for the last two days.

Mike: What's the matter?

Angela: A mosquito bit me when I was traveling and I have a high fever now.

Mike: You should go to the hospital immediately. It may be something serious.

Brad: What's up with you, Ben?

Ben: I'm feeling a bit sick, that's all.

Brad: Why don't you drink a glass of water slowly? It may work.

Ben: OK, I'll try it.

LANGUAGE IN ACTION 4. Track 5. page 127

I had a beautiful figure when I was younger because I used to pay attention to everything I ate. Now I'm not as thin as I used to be. I got married and had two kids. Sometimes I don't even pay attention to the way I look at all.

Glossary

A

acclaimed aclamado(a), consagrado(a)
account conta
acrylic acrílico
actually na verdade
acute agudo(a)
advice conselho
advise aconselhar
afford poder pagar
against contra
ageing envelhecimento
aim visar, almejar
alliance aliança, união
although embora
amount porção, quantidade
antioxidant antioxidante
apologize desculpar-se
appeal apelar, atrair
appoint nomear, designar
architect arquiteto(a)
argue discutir, argumentar
arrest prender
arrive chegar
arthritis artrite
as long as desde que
ask perguntar; pedir
assessment avaliação
attempt tentar
attend participar; assistir
avoid evitar

B

background experiência
bakery padaria
bariatric surgery cirurgia bariátrica
basket cesta, cesto
battle batalha
beacon luz; farol, sinal
beef carne bovina
beg implorar
behavior comportamento
benefit benefício
besides além de
birthplace local de nascimento
bless abençoar
blind cego(a)
blow rajada de vento
blue-eyed de olhos azuis
boast vangloriar-se
boil ferver
booming estrondoso(a)
bored entediado(a)
bravery bravura
break intervalo
breakdown colapso
bring up criar; educar
broke sem dinheiro
bully intimidar, ameaçar
bullying intimidação, coação
burn off queimar
business negócio

C

cease cessar
challenge desafiar, contestar; desafio
charter school escola independente das regras que se aplicam às escolas públicas tradicionais
cheat trair
chemistry química
chicken pox catapora
chronic crônico(a)
chubby rechonchudo(a)
citizen cidadão(ã)
citizenship cidadania
clever inteligente
climb escalar
cocoa cacau
coherent coerente
compliance conformidade
concerned preocupado(a)
confidence confiança, segurança
constipation constipação
consulting firm firma de consultoria

consumption consumo
cop policial
costume fantasia
counsel aconselhar
course percurso
customer cliente

D

damage dano, estrago
daydream devaneio; sonhar acordado(a)
decrease diminuir
defeat derrotar
degree grau
dejection depressão, desânimo
demanding exigente
deny negar
derision escárnio, deboche
develop desenvolver
diarrhea diarreia
disabled deficiente
donor doador(a)
downfall derrocada, ruína
draw desenhar
drought seca
drugstore farmácia
dry seco(a)
due que deve ser entregue
due to devido a
duty dever

E

educated culto(a), instruído(a)
elf elfo
enchant encantar, seduzir
endangered em perigo, em risco
environment ambiente
epidemic epidemia
epistle epístola
eradicate erradicar
essay ensaio
ethical ético, moral
excuse desculpa
expertise especialidade, conhecimento

F

fabric tecido
fail reprovar, fracassar
faint desmaiar
fast-talk persuadir, convencer
feature traço, característica
fed up with farto de, cansado de
fictitious fictício
fire demitir
flaw falha, defeito
float flutuar
flu gripe, *influenza*
fluidity fluidez
flunk ser reprovado(a)
folks família, parentes
folly tolice, insensatez
forgive perdoar

G

gain ganhar, ganho (subst.)
gastritis gastrite
genes gene
genocide genocídio
genre gênero
germ germe
get carried away deixar-se levar
get fired ser demitido(a)
get in shape ficar em forma
go through passar por
grab segurar, agarrar
gratitude gratidão
gun down balear

H

handkerchief lenço
handle lidar
hand-made feito manualmente, artesanalmente
hang enforcar
health saúde
health insurance seguro-saúde
heart-breaking de partir o coração
heat aquecer
heel salto de sapato
help ajudar; evitar
heritage patrimônio
highlight realçar, destacar
hobgoblin diabrete
host anfitrião
house hospedar, abrigar
however contudo

I

illiterate analfabeto(a)
illness doença
impair prejudicar
impairment deficiência
impeccable impecável
impoverished miserável
improve aperfeiçoar, aprimorar
in a hurry com pressa
in spite of a despeito de
incidence incidência
increase aumentar
increasingly cada vez mais
infer supor, deduzir, inferir
infirmity enfermidade
inhabitant habitante, morador(a)
iron passar a ferro
issue questão

J

join filiar-se
journal periódico
judge julgar, juiz (subst.)

K

kite pipa
knock bater (à porta)
knock it off pare com isso!

L

label etiqueta, rótulo
land pousar, aterrissar
landscape paisagem, visão, ponto de vista
large grande
laughter riso
law lei
lawyer advogado(a)
lead levar a, conduzir
leather couro
left-handed canhoto(a)
legend lenda
leisure lazer
lessen diminuir
level-headed equilibrado(a)
library biblioteca
lie situar-se
lift carona
lift up levantar, suspender
light bulb lâmpada
limerick poema humorístico de cinco versos
line fila
liposuction lipoaspiração
lock trancar
lone solitário(a), solteiro(a)
look after cuidar
look forward estar ansioso(a) para
lousy muito ruim
lunch almoço
lush luxuriante

M

mail enviar
makeup maquiagem
manage controlar, gerenciar, administrar
mandatory obrigatório(a)
manufacture fabricar, confeccionar
match wits iniciar competição intelectual
mayor prefeito(a)
melt derreter
memoir memórias
metabolism metabolismo
method método
middle-aged de meia-idade
midnight meia-noite
mind importar-se
moist úmido(a)
moonlit enluarado(a)
moonshine divagação
mortgage hipoteca
muscle músculo

N

nevertheless apesar disso
NGO (non-governmental organization) ONG (organização não governamental)
non-profit sem fins lucrativos

O

obese obeso(a)
obey obedecer
obtain obter
oil petróleo
on account of por conta de
once uma vez que
otitis otite

outnumber exceder, ser de maior número que
over and over again repetidamente
overview panorama, perspectiva
overweight acima do peso
own próprio(a)

P

painkiller analgésico
pandemic pandemia
paraplegic paraplégico(a)
parent pai, mãe
path caminho, trajeto
peel casca
perhaps talvez
philanthropist filantropo
philanthropy filantropia
pick on criticar
play a large role ter um papel importante
play tag brincar de pega-pega
pleasure prazer
plight dilema, problema
plod on caminhar ou fazer algo lentamente
plot enredo, trama
plumber encanador, bombeiro hidráulico
plump roliço(a), gorducho(a)
poetry poesia
portray retratar
pour despejar, derramar
pray rezar, orar
preamble preâmbulo
pregnant grávida
prejudice preconceito
pressure pressão
pretend fingir
prevalence prevalência
prevalent prevalente, predominante
prevent prevenir, evitar
priestess sacerdotisa
private particular, privado(a)
profit-making com fins lucrativos
prominent proeminente, notável
provide providenciar, fornecer
publish publicar
puppy cachorrinho
pursue seguir, perseguir
push empurrar

Q

qualify qualificar-se, capacitar-se

R

railroad ferrovia
rarely raramente
rate taxa
rather than em vez de
receipt comprovante, recibo
receive receber
recognition reconhecimento
regard considerar
relative parente
remain permanecer
remainder remanescente
remote remoto(a), distante
reparation reparação
replicate replicar, repetir
require requerer, exigir
rescue socorrer, resgatar, salvar
research pesquisar
researcher pesquisador(a)
retire aposentar-se
reveal revelar
reverberate ecoar
rhyme rimar
risky perigoso(a), arriscado(a)
rite rito
robber ladrão
roof telhado
rule regra, regulamento
ruling governante, dirigente
run gerenciar, administrar

S

sacred sagrado(a)
sanctioning sanção
save salvar
scorn desdém, desprezo
screen tela
seaside costa, litoral, beira-mar
season temporada
seasonal periódico(a)
server garçom, garçonete
shout gritar
shower banho, chuveiro
signal sinalizar
single único(a)
skip rope pular corda
skull crânio
slam bater com força

slide escorregador
smart esperto(a), inteligente
soft-hearted coração mole
somber sombrio(a)
sore ferida
sponsor patrocinar
spotting localização, identificação
spread espalhar, divulgar
sprinkle polvilhar
spur encorajar
stable estável
stage encenar; palco
stand suportar
standing prestígio
stanza estrofe
stare olhar fixamente
stereotype estereótipo
stick to manter
stoppage paralisação, suspensão
stranger desconhecido(a), estranho(a)
strength força
stretching alongamento
strict rígido(a), severo(a)
strike greve
striking impactante
strong-willed obstinado(a)
struggle lutar, batalhar
stuffy abafado(a), mal ventilado(a)
succeed ter bom êxito, ter sucesso
surgery cirurgia
survey pesquisa, enquete
swear jurar
swine flu gripe suína
syllogism silogismo
synergy sinergia

T

take-away para viagem
tale conto
tax imposto, tributo
temples têmporas
therapist terapeuta
thick-skinned insensível
thought pensamento
threaten ameaçar
thriving próspero(a)
throne trono
throughout por todo(a)
tidy arrumado(a), organizado(a)
tissue tecido
tone-deaf desafinado(a)
touch tocar
tough difícil
transaction transação, operação
troop tropa
trouble problema, encrenca
truth verdade
tutor educar
type digitar

U

ulcer úlcera
unemployed desempregado(a)
unlike diferentemente de
upset perturbar

V

vesicle vesicular
vulnerable vulnerável

W

warn advertir, avisar
warrant garantir
water regar
wave acenar
weatherman homem ou mulher do tempo (noticiário)
weight peso
well-paid bem pago
wheel roda
wheelchair cadeira de rodas
whereas ao passo que
width largura
withdrawal retrocesso, recuo
workaholic viciado(a) em trabalho
worldwide mundial
wrap embrulhar

Y

youth juventude

Irregular Verbs List

Infinitive	Past	Past Participle	Translation
awake	awoke	awoken	acordar, estar acordado
be (am/is/are)	was/were	been	ser, estar
bear	bore	borne (Br) born (Am)	suportar, sustentar
beat	beat	beaten	vencer, derrotar
become	became	become	tornar-se, passar a ser
begin	began	begun	começar, iniciar
bind	bound	bound	ligar; encadernar; contratar
bite	bit	bitten	morder, picar
blow	blew	blown	soprar; tocar (instrumento de sopro)
break	broke	broken	quebrar, partir
bring	brought	brought	trazer
build	built	built	construir
burn	burnt burned	burnt (Br) burned (Am)	queimar, arder
buy	bought	bought	comprar
catch	caught	caught	pegar, apanhar, agarrar
choose	chose	chosen	escolher, selecionar
come	came	come	vir
cost	cost	cost	custar
creep	crept	crept	rastejar; arrastar-se
cut	cut	cut	cortar
deal	dealt	dealt	tratar, lidar com
dig	dug	dug	cavar
do (do/does)	did	done	fazer
draw	drew	drawn	desenhar
dream	dreamt dreamed	dreamt (Br) dreamed (Am)	sonhar; desejar, planejar
drink	drank	drunk	beber
drive	drove	driven	dirigir, guiar; conduzir
eat	ate	eaten	comer
fall	fell	fallen	cair, baixar
feed	fed	fed	alimentar(-se); suprir
feel	felt	felt	sentir

fight	fought	fought	lutar, brigar
fly	flew	flown	voar; pilotar
forget	forgot	forgotten	esquecer
forgive	forgave	forgiven	perdoar, desculpar
get	got	got (Br) / gotten (Am)	receber, obter, conseguir
give	gave	given	dar
go	went	gone	ir
grind	ground	ground	moer; pulverizar
grow	grew	grown	crescer; cultivar
have (have/has)	had	had	ter
hear	heard	heard	ouvir
hide	hid	hidden	esconder(-se), ocultar(-se)
hit	hit	hit	bater
hold	held	held	prender, segurar, agarrar-se a; aguentar; sediar
hold down	held down	held down	segurar
hurt	hurt	hurt	ferir; machucar(-se)
know	knew	known	saber; conhecer
lead	led	led	levar, conduzir
learn	learnt learned	learnt (Br) learned (Am)	aprender
leave	left	left	sair, deixar, partir, ir embora; abandonar
lend	lent	lent	emprestar
lose	lost	lost	perder
make	made	made	fazer, criar, produzir
mean	meant	meant	significar, querer dizer
meet	met	met	encontrar(-se)
overcome	overcame	overcame	superar
oversee	oversaw	overseen	fiscalizar; conferir
put	put	put	pôr, colocar
quit	quit	quit	deixar; partir; abandonar; desistir
read	read	read	ler
redo	redid	redone	refazer
rethink	rethought	rethought	repensar, rever uma ideia
rewrite	rewrote	rewritten	reescrever
rid	rid	rid	livrar(-se)
ride	rode	ridden	montar, cavalgar, andar de
rise	rose	risen	surgir, subir, erguer; levantar(-se)
run	ran	run	correr, conduzir, dirigir (negócio)
see	saw	seen	ver, enxergar